SCHOOL WORSHIP
An Obituary

School Worship

An Obituary

JOHN M HULL

SCM PRESS LTD

334 01460 3

First published 1975 by SCM Press Ltd
56 Bloomsbury Street WC1

© SCM Press Ltd 1975

Typeset by Specialised Offset Services Ltd, Liverpool
and printed in Great Britain by
Fletcher & Son Ltd, Norwich

To my father and mother

Contents

Foreword

This book is based on a series of lectures given at the 1972 Conference in Sydney of the Committee for Religious Education of the Australian Headmasters' Conference. I am grateful to the Committee for the opportunity this gave me to reconsider some of these problems and for their encouragement in turning the series into a book. The book, like the lectures, deals with the situation in England and Wales, but I hope it will not be entirely without relevance in Australia where religious education is passing through a period of rapid development. I would also like to thank Mrs Sally Ginns of the Birmingham University School of Education for the patient skill with which she typed the manuscript. Parts of chapters 4 and 6 previously appeared in a shorter form in the *Journal of Curriculum Studies*, Vol. 1, 1969, pp. 208-18 and in *Educational Review*, Vol. 23, 1972, pp.59-68.

This is only a slight book, and some readers may be surprised to know that it has taken me ten years to write it. My dawning realization of the critical nature of the problems confronting the school assembly goes back to 1962 when I began teaching in London and trying to organize ten school assemblies every week. My fellow religious education teachers in Britain will understand why it took so long to write so little. The theoretical and practical problems of school worship are considerable and although I do not believe I have solved all of them I hope what I have to say will contribute to the sharing of experiences and views which is the main way progress is possible in this area.

This has been a hard book for a Christian to write. It is sad to have to record the epitaph to hopes the direct Christianization of the county schools through worship, hopes which were so high in Christian teachers' hearts years ago. They were not wrong to attempt it, but we would be wrong to try to continue it in just the same way. And yet I am still foolish enough to believe that if we can understand them correctly in relation to each other, Christianity and education may still be partners, and in that partnership there may yet be the seeds of a cultural revolution.

July 1974   John M. Hull

1 *Worship in the County School 1870-1965*

Before 1870 nearly all schools in England and Wales were church schools. Religious observances, as they were called,[1] usually took place every day. The syllabus of religious instruction used in such schools was really a catechism, and since the catechism would contain items such as the Ten Commandments, the Lord's Prayer and the Apostles' Creed, it supplied the needs both of instruction and worship. Indeed, if by a syllabus we mean materials arranged in order according to grade levels, then liturgies for use in schools are as old or older than syllabuses. The schools did not worship in order to reinforce the instruction; they instructed in order to facilitate the worship. Children memorized the main items of the daily service.

Daily, or Sunday Services for Church Schools for Poor Children[2] is typical of the many aids for the conduct of school prayers which circulated in the middle nineteenth century. The service set out in the leaflet is for children in the sense that it refers to them and is intended to be used in their presence. Prayer is offered for 'the poor children of this school' and reference is made to the fatherless, but no concession is made at all to the religious conceptions which children might have. Prayers mention Christ's infancy and boyhood but are not couched in simple language.

It was thus unthinkable that the state schools created after the 1870 Act should be 'godless'. In 1878 a government circular asked the School Boards whether 'any religious observance or religious instruction' was 'practiced or given' in the schools under their management. Details of any regulations governing these religious practices were to be supplied.[3] Only sixty-five School Boards reported that no

religious observances at all were held in their schools. A
further circular[4] questioned them more closely, since it was
thought that the original question about religious observance
might not have been fully understood. The questions now
asked were: 'Are any hymns or prayers used in the Board
Schools?' and 'Is the Bible read in the Schools (with or
without comment thereon)?'

The replies to this second circular reduced the number of
'secular' Boards from sixty-five to forty-nine and there
remained eleven Boards which gave no return.

The returns indicate that in very many maintained schools
at this time there was, as in the church schools, little or no
distinction between worship and religious instruction. Many
Boards allowed or required their schools to hear the reading
of the Bible for twenty or thirty minutes at the beginning of
every day, or before the children went home for lunch.
Prayers, read by the teacher or extempore, often accompanied the Bible reading. Often the Board regulations stated
that the schools could use 'the prayer known as the Lord's
Prayer and no other'. This would be read to the school at the
beginning of each day. Some schools both opened and closed
the day with prayers and hymns, others sang a hymn only at
the close of the day, other Board returns make no mention of
hymns at all. Sometimes there is control over which hymns
are to be used. The instruction of the Reading Board was that
the hymn is 'to be selected by the teacher from the book
known as *Curwen's Child's Own Hymn Book* but other more
enterprising Boards compiled their own hymn books. A few
Boards specifically declared that 'no religious hymns shall be
sung or used in the schools'.

Practices regarding the prayers were equally varied. Sometimes a school had to write out the form of prayer it
proposed to use and submit it to the Board for approval.
Sometimes the collects and the General Confession from the
Book of Common Prayer were prescribed. Often the Lord's
Prayer, the Apostles' Creed and the Ten Commandments, all
having been memorized, would be recited by the school
together. The religious instruction consisted in the memorization and sometimes the explanation of these.

In many of the regulations governing worship and instruction there was a kind of strict neutrality. The teacher was

told that it might include 'the history of the Jews and the Jewish nation and the geography and natural history of Ancient as well as Modern Palestine; but that in any use which may be made of the Bible in teaching or illustrating these subjects, it is to be distinctly understood that no reference whatever is to be made to the doctrines taught therein; except in cases of discipline and to enforce moral teaching'.[5] This can hardly be called religious instruction except in the sense that it implied the belief that the repetition by heart of prayers and the listening to the Bible would produce beneficial results. This sort of thing is very different from the spirit of the 1920s and 1930s. The schools did not become doctrinaire until the advent of the Agreed Syllabuses. Not all Boards, however, allowed fears of denomi-nationalism to lead to a completely non-committal attitude towards religion. Llanfairtalhaiarn required 'that the school-master be instructed to confine his explanation of the Bible to the great and simple truths of Christianity, avoiding all sectarian and dogmatic teaching'.[6] In Llangwick, Glamorgan-shire, they used neither prayer nor any reading from the Bible but only the hymns of Sankey and Moody.

The Return of 1906[7] does not indicate any great changes, except that syllabus details are more frequently given. In Cheshire the aims were moral and spiritual development and there were hymns and prayers both morning and evening. This is a common pattern. But quite often nothing is said of worship and Hereford replied that not only was no council syllabus provided but the authority did not know what its schools were doing and had no information at all on these matters.[8]

The Tractarian movement seems to have had some influence in the Church of England schools in increasing the use of the Book of Common Prayer during the latter part of the nineteenth century, but by and large it remained true that Christian education was thought of as mainly be-havioural (devotions, liturgies, recitations) and perhaps cerebral (creed and catechism).[9]

In looking to the official syllabuses of the churches and the county schools to discover their practices and expect-ations regarding worship one must remember that the major function of the syllabuses was to make inspection of the

schools possible. The syllabuses with their lists of hymns and
prayers were in fact often directed towards the inspectors
rather than towards the teachers. The series of syllabuses
produced by the Diocese of Oxford from 1875 to 1926
illustrates the trends clearly.[10] Not until the 1918 edition do
we read 'the aim of the Inspectorate is to encourage the
school and help the Teachers'.[11] Worship was still thought of
as indistinguishable from instruction, as the ten pages of
'observances' which preface the 1918 edition indicate.

Another rather typical example of the identification of
worship with instruction and training is found in the syllabus
of the National Society which was published around the turn
of the century.[12] This falls into two parts, the first being
'Scripture History' and the second 'Catechism'. 'The teacher
is reminded that a thorough knowledge of the Creeds, Lord's
Prayer, and Ten Commandments, will be of the highest
possible value to the child in after life, and that therefore no
pains should be spared in order to make the child master
thoroughly — first, their words; second, their meanings; and
third some of the texts which refer to them'.[13] Almost the
only comment on method deals with the need for repetition,
which must be separate (i.e. one child at a time) and distinct.
It is in the repetition required for the memorization of these
items that the worship of the children would take place and
at the same time their readiness to be examined by the
inspectors would be checked.

Religious teaching and worship in the home had the same
characteristics. The little four-page syllabus for parents issued
by the Diocese of London in 1908[14] divides the child's
knowledge and devotional exercises into six parts. The first
part, 'What he should know by heart' consists, for the
six-year-old, of the Gloria, the Lord's Prayer and the orders
of morning and evening prayer from the Book of Common
Prayer together with one or two simple hymns. The second
part of the syllabus is 'liturgical knowledge' and this consists
of the events associated with the festivals of the church and
the child is expected to be able to find his way around the
Prayer Book. The object of instruction in the home is thus to
enable the child to participate in the public worship of the
church and there is no distinction between the training in
words and actions which this required and the rest of the

catechetical and historical material.

A profound change came over school worship during the early 1920s when the new religious education arose,[15] a force which was to dominate religion in the British school with unprecedented power for forty years, coming to its climax and triumph in the passing of the 1944 Education Act which for the first time made school worship obligatory. Now the word 'worship' begins to take the place of the word 'observances' and 'the duties of personal and corporate religion' take the place of the formal teaching of liturgy and ecclesiastical practices without regard for the spiritual growth of the individual.

The 1921 Winchester Syllabus is a fine example of the new trends.[16] The aim of the syllabus is 'to give instruction in the Christian faith as a living thing, with power over daily life: to put in right proportion the teaching of the necessary formularies, and to avoid the impression that Christian knowledge consists in committing to memory a mass of details'.[17] Here for the first time we have syllabuses with distinctive theological purposes. 'We have tried to bring out in simple ways the theological and religious significance of the Person of Christ'.[18] The syllabus is now no longer a guide to the inspectorate or to the work to be memorized (and thus to be examined) but a guide to the teacher, and so includes a series of notes on various aspects of religious education, lists of usable hymns, remarks about the use of the syllabus in different kinds of schools and so on. This is an early form of the short essays which the statutory Agreed Syllabuses were to use to introduce and follow their actual content, advisory essays which in the 1970s supplanted the syllabuses themselves.[19]

The new attitudes towards school worship are seen in the Winchester recommendation that classroom worship should take place daily and for the whole school at least once a week. But there is no insistence upon systematic memorization. 'Prayers will be learned by praying and hymns by singing.'[20]

The growth of the ecumenical movement, the decline of denominational suspicion, the rise of modern liberal theology — all these factors contributed to the rejection of the rigid neutrality and the careful formality which dominated school worship during earlier decades. The 1921 Winchester syllabus suggests study of 'other parts of Christ's church' and goes on to mention the Roman Catholics, the Eastern Orthodox, the non-episcopal communions, concluding with the church universal and the sorrow of divisions.[21]

These new trends, first found in the church schools, soon appeared in the council schools as well. Religious education gained in confidence. The Macmillan Syllabus of 1923 remarks, 'Why should not the *tone* of the religious instruction period be carried over into all the other lessons?'[22] The use of the word 'religious' as an adjective to describe the ethos of the whole education offered by the school was to become typical of the new religious education. We find here the same move in emphasis, from mere recitation of memorized prayer. There should be teaching 'children *to pray* in addition to teaching them *to say prayers*'.[23] The progress in child-centred method which this important syllabus made is seen in the advice that prayer, for young children, should arise out of the subject of the lessons, and children should be encouraged to make their own prayers. The theological coherence of religious education is shown by the fact that the history and geography of the Bible are now taught not to avoid Christian doctrine but in order to deepen the impression of the historical context in which the divine revelation took place. ' . . . there will be greater attention than previously to geography and contemporary history so that there is gained an increasingly intelligent knowledge of the revelation of God to Man'.[24]

It was the famous Cambridgeshire Syllabus of 1924 which brought out for the first time the explicit role of the school assembly in the new religious education. The Cambridgeshire Syllabus was the result of the work of an Advisory Committee appointed by the Education Committee in 1923 consisting of representatives of the Church of England, the Free Churches and the teaching profession with a secretary provided by the Education Committee itself. The object of the exercise was to try to resolve the problem of the dual system, whereby schools maintained by the churches and the local authority existed together in the same area, by providing an agreed syllabus 'of Religious Instruction and observance which would be acceptable to all religious bodies and would form an integral part of the educational system of all schools'.[25] If this could be achieved, then further steps in the integrating of the two systems might follow.

The syllabus opens with a sixteen page article called 'The Teaching of Religion'. The opening words are 'The ambition of teachers is enlarged of late. No longer are they content to impart information.' What teachers now aspire towards is the full teaching of religion, in all its inspirational and revelatory power. This will be done mainly on a basis of the Bible as a religious book, held together by the theology of progressive revelation. 'Schools have proved that they can be the ideal nurseries of the new biblical learning.'[26] What would issue from this would be no barren instruction, no mere setting out of historical and archaeological facts. Rather, '. . . the Syllabus is a guide to prayer and praise'. The beauty and majesty of the divine revelation would again ring out in the schools.

To appreciate the significance of this opening essay we must go back more than fifty years into the debates which preceded the passing of the 1870 Education Act. The discussions about the possibility of providing religious teaching in the schools which the state was about to provide offer many interesting illustrations of the problems created for instruction when co-operation between those who differed in their views was contemplated. To the rigid denominationalists, co-operation would destroy the possibility of instruction.[27]

In 1865 John Hubbard, Anglican Member of Parliament, discussed the problems raised by the condition under which the state gave aid to church schools, namely, that children of dissenters attending Church of England schools in receipt of state funds should not be subject to Church of England teaching.[28] This condition was known as the 'conscience clause'. Hubbard maintains that in view of the contributions made by the church towards these schools, the schools do have the right to offer church teaching to all their pupils, even to the children of dissenters. Agreement with the conscience clause would not be possible for an Anglican priest since it would not be compatible with his view of his duty to the children in his parish. '. . . he offers freely his own efforts to the instruction of his people, and he only asks in return that his conscience be not offended or his independence coerced by giving to those who disclaim his ministrations a legal right to demand from him what he could give only by violating his conscience and surrendering his independence.'[29]

The implication is that one could not expect a clergyman to give information about Christianity which is merely factual, or to give any information at all about other types of Christianity than his own. It would be against the conscience of the Anglican clergyman to permit any child not to be instructed in the precepts of the Church of England and it simply did not occur to anyone that the Anglican clergyman might offer a course on non-conformity to everyone. The assumption is that Anglicans do not want to know about the dissenters, and vice versa, and that the church school is not the place for them to learn this anyway.

These difficulties are thought by Hubbard to make it impossible to have a National Education System, since this would either have to be completely secular or it would have to compromise the conscience of the clergy by at least offering a 'conscience clause' to dissenters. Hubbard rejects the idea that the Creeds, the Lord's Prayer and the Decalogue might be taught but not the Catechism, on the grounds that the Catechism is only a summary of the rest and that the teaching of the Church of England is one and indivisible.

Here we see how instruction and proselytizing zeal have swamped the conception of education. We also see the sort of atmosphere out of which the traditions of state religious instruction grew and the way in which the religious syllabuses in state schools of the period after 1870 were formed.

The conscience clause discussed by Hubbard was the forerunner of the Cowper-Temple clause in the Forster Act, 1870, which forbad the teaching of any formulary or catechism distinctive of a denomination. The earlier conscience clause in Church of England schools receiving state aid forbad the teaching to the children of dissenters of 'the doctrine or formularies of the Church'. Hubbard argued from this that it followed that there could be no teaching of religion at all, since a churchman will not admit any difference 'between the vital doctrines of Christianity and the distinctive doctrines of the Church'.[30] Even unadorned Bible lessons contain matter which is part of the doctrine of the church, therefore in the Church of England schools where the conscience clause is insisted upon and in all the schools of any possible National System there could be teaching of neither Bible, doctrine nor religion.

It is against this background that the significance of the Cambridgeshire Syllabus of 1924 must be interpreted. The opening heading 'The Teaching of Religion' is original, bold and striking. There has been a fear that 'religion would depart from schools if the safeguards and supremacies, the social training of its teachers, the dependence on church or chapel, were interfered with. There was contest; then weariness of contest; then gradual discovery that religion within a good school was a pervasive influence; that religion could be taught with the painstaking of science; and that secular studies were actions of religion and thus were romantic and serviceable'.[3][1] This article, often reprinted in later Agreed Syllabuses, is the answer of the Agreed Syllabuses to the charge that inter-denominational co-operation would destroy the possibility of *instructing* in Christianity and to the consequent claim that religion could only be taught in religiously sponsored schools. This is also part of the significance of the famous declaration in the same syllabus. 'All Education rightly conceived is religious education.'[3][2] The Cambridgeshire Syllabus of 1924 was thus the manifesto of the state school as an agent of Christian nurture.

Following the syllabus proper, there is a concluding essay of two pages called 'Religion and Corporate Life in the School', followed by comments on hymns, and a small collection of recommended prayers. This essay is the found-ation of the idea of worship in the period of the Agreed Syllabuses. It has been reprinted, quoted, adapted, enlarged and abridged countless times in the syllabuses and its influence can still be traced today.

The message of this little essay is that 'we cannot narrow religious teaching down to the limits of a syllabus', but that every subject and indeed the whole life of the school has implications for Christian nurture and the development of character. To discover the nature of the school as a Christian community, questions must be asked about the prefect system, the forms of competition encouraged in the school, the service performed by pupils for each other and the community, and the increased ability of pupils to be guided by their own consciences and their own reasoning in living the responsible life.

Only at the conclusion is there a reference to the 'Morning Assembly' which 'will be welcomed as the opportunity for the dedication of all the school life and work'. This is all that is said specifically on the subject of school worship, except for a sentence advising a varied choice of prayers and a comment on hymn singing.

An interesting picture of the development of concepts of worship and nurture in the state school emerges if we compare the 1924 syllabus with the 1939 edition.[33]

Since by 1939 the rationale of the state school as a vehicle of Christian nurture with worship at its centre had evolved more fully and gathered confidence, the 1939 Syllabus presents a less liberal appearance than the 1924 Syllabus. The earlier syllabus required all teaching to be 'infused with a sense of earnest enquiry', but the 1939 revision omits this expression and substitutes 'infused with the appreciation of goodness, beauty and truth'. In 1924 the child was said to learn by doing; in 1939 this is interpreted within a framework of the all-encompassing guidance offered by the school. The 1924 version is addressed to 'companions in the teaching profession', but the later one says that its precepts should be 'constantly before the Headmaster or Head-mistress'. The 1924 syllabus speaks of the evils of 'emulation and competition' but this is changed later to encouraging 'proper forms of competition'. The awkward question about whether prefectorial systems train little tyrants is omitted altogether in 1939, as is the advice about helping the pupil to submerge his individual desire to excel, and instead of life abounding as a mark of inspiration (1924) we are now teaching the grace of courtesy. The 1939 additions are as important as the omissions. A long statement about the responsibility of the teacher in moulding the spirituality of the child is added and the 1924 paragraph about autonomy in ethics is replaced by a paragraph dealing with the Christian doctrinal basis of ethics and discipline. The utilitarian optimism of 1924 ('When every child thinks first of the common good and controls himself with that end in view') is replaced by Christian ethics ('Without faith in the Father, the brotherhood of man is left without foundation') and the brotherhood of man is 'the charter of the common good . . .'. Perhaps the two most symptomatic features of the changed outlook in 1939 are what can be called the democratic omission and the christological addition. The democratic omission is the final paragraph of the 1924 syllabus on 'Religion in the School', which is left out in 1939. The crucial part of the paragraph reads: 'Every teacher knows how we learn by teaching; he knows it better than his father did. Authority gave way to teaching, and today teaching gives way to conversation.' This remarkable sentence, with its progressive and even radical implications, was never to see the light of day in any subsequent syllabus. The christological addition is the expansion of the concluding paragraph of the 1924 essay on 'Religion and Corporate Life' which refers to the example of Jesus Christ. The idea of Jesus 'who himself adopted the life of a Teacher' is dropped (it was apparently not considered a sufficiently distinctive idea of Jesus) and this sentence is added, referring to the teacher's role: 'And he can pass on to his pupils no greater or more lasting gift than to quicken their admiration of that unique personality, and to fill them with the desire to know Him better, to be like Him, and to work in His service.'

When we come to the section dealing with assembly, the changes in 1939 are quite dramatic. We now have a new major heading 'Corporate Prayer' and in place of the nine lines given to the subject in 1924 we have now five pages of detailed comment followed by several further pages of practical advice and resources. The tendency in 1939 is to emphasize the communal and ethos building aspects of corporate prayer. The later syllabus adds a lengthy paragraph about the importance of the teacher's own example in prayer and explains the nature of Christian prayer in some detail. This was to become a favourite in later syllabuses and is repeated, sometimes acknowledged, sometimes simply included without comment, time and time again. References to corporate religious observances abound in the 1939 syllabus itself. There is a discussion about 'the practice and enjoyment of religious observances' with junior children;[34] a course on 'Prayer' is added for children aged nine and over[35] and a worship course for pupils aged fourteen and over.[36]

Finally, it is interesting and significant that whereas the 1924 syllabus opens with the essay 'The Teaching of Religion' and concludes with the essay 'Religion and Corporate Life in the School', the 1939 syllabus reverses this order. 'The Teaching of Religion' is now much abbreviated and appears in 1939 simply as the fifth of seven appendices. But the essay on 'Corporate Life' is much expanded, as we have seen, and occupies pride of place as the first major part of the syllabus. The possibility of really teaching religion had been established by 1939. The previous fifteen years had seen that accomplished. Now the task was to strengthen the Christian character of the school as a whole, both in its general atmosphere but particularly in its daily worship.

The final stage of the development of Agreed Syllabus religion is marked by the appearance of the third edition of the Cambridgeshire syllabus in 1949. Ten years have gone by. A world war has been fought and won. The new Education Act has set the seal on all that Christians had sought to do in education since 1924. The 1949 syllabus is a mature work, characterized by a statesmanlike outlook. The 1924 style was idyllic and rhapsodic; in 1939 it was flowery and rhetorical; in 1949 it is calm and measured.

In place of the 1939 introduction of six pages by J.S. Whale of Cheshunt College we find a nine page anonymous statement about the Christian faith in the post-war world, its role with respect to communism and democracy, and the tasks confronting the school and the Christian educator in the light of the 1944 Act. There is a strong stress on social and political action in the reconstruction of the world. The 1939 introduction was also about civilization and its redemption, but Whale had said considerably more about the Bible, teaching the Bible and the power of that teaching to renovate the schools and thus the nation. The 1949 introduction says little about education or religious education, but surveys the international scene from a great height. It speaks from the pinnacle of achievement and vision. There is no longer any need to argue about religion in the school. The task is now global.

The essay 'The Teaching of Religion', already relegated to the back as a minor appendix in 1939, is dropped altogether in 1949. This battle has long since been won. Only the 1939 subheading 'Religion in the School' is retained and now it is used for the title of the essay which opened the 1939 syllabus, then called 'Religion and the Corporate life of the School'. In 1949 the heading 'School Worship' replaced the heading 'Corporate Prayer' and thus the contemporary terminology was established. There is, however, little or no development in the concept of school worship between 1939 and 1949, certainly nothing like the changes between 1924 and 1939. More practical advice is given in 1949, for example the section on the conduct of the infants' 'Morning Ring',[37] and the section on prayer for juniors is much enlarged.[38]

But the thinking about the religious ethos of the school has developed considerably in 1949. The first part of the article now called 'Religion in the School' is completely rewritten as an expansion of the sentence: 'All education rightly conceived is religious education.' This is now explained in terms of the capacity of religion and religion alone to deal with 'the proper end of man' which must underlie all education. The view of man expressed in the school must therefore be a function of its view of religion and in a Christian school the Christian view of man will prevail. It is in this sense that education is to be religious. This was not, however, interpreted in a generally humanitarian sense nor in the light of more recent ideas of the nature of education. It served instead to reinforce the nurturing aim. This is elaborated in many places in the 1949 syllabus. 'While the teacher should teach, and not preach, in the classroom, he should have an ever-present sense of responsibility that by his teaching children may be "lead into the way of truth".'[39]

We are now in a position to summarize the philosophy (for it was becoming so self-conscious and coherent a set of attitudes and beliefs that it can now be called a philosophy) of religious education which held sway from about 1920 until about 1965 in schools.

1. The school was regarded as a Christian community.
2. The task of Christian education (which was not distinguished from religious education and which was an attitude towards the whole curriculum as well as belonging to specific periods) was to bring this community to

self-consciousness, that is to create Christian discipleship.
3. Religious education can as a consequence only be taught
by Christians.
4. In assembly, the school affirmed explicitly what was
implicit in all of its work, namely its aspiration towards
the divine society of which it was the image. The school
would lift its heart in worship of God.

The clauses in the 1944 Education Act dealing with school
worship were warmly welcomed by all concerned with
religious education. The seal had been set on more than
twenty years of religious expansion in the schools. 'Now, and
for the years to come, nothing less than the repeal of section
twenty-five of the Education Act 1944 . . . can prevent the
daily offering to Almighty God of the worship of the school
children of England and Wales. Meanwhile, "the voice of
prayer is never silent, nor dies the strain of praise away".'[40]
'I believe we ought to regard the Act as a great victory for
Christian principles — a sure and certain proof that the work
of the Churches has not been such a failure as many people
represent it to be.'[41] The Oxford Diocesan Council of
Education was one of many such bodies to express approval
in only slightly less lyrical tones. 'This new recognition by
the state of the vital importance of worship in the life of
every school within the statutory system is a landmark in
English history, for it indicates that the lead which the
Church has for centuries been giving in her own schools is
now to be followed in those of the many local authorities.'[42]
The literature on school worship which followed the 1944
Act reveals little appreciation of the distinction between the
church school and the state school and no qualms of
conscience whatever about compulsion. *The Oxford Book of
School Worship*, the earlier editions of which have already
been discussed, was revised in 1958 with the 1944 Act in
mind and offered to both church and state schools. But, as
the Bishop of Oxford says, 'the substance (of the revised
edition) remains the same'.[43] It is assumed that all pupils
taking part in the assembly will be convinced Christians. Of
the Apostles' Creed, 'the utmost care should be taken that,
when it is used, it should be said by everyone as an act of
faith, and in such distinct and reverential tone that every

word can be heard'.[44] Pupils are to give thanks for their
baptism and confirmation, prayers are offered for the
extension of the church, for 'our bishops and clergy' and so
on.[45] It is assumed that the religious life of the school has as
one of its functions the service òf the church. 'The aim in
selecting prayers for this book has been to give the pupils
such contact with the Book of Common Prayer that they
may come to love it . . .'[46] and ' . . . the school prayers
should lead naturally to a devout appreciation of the public
services of the church'.[47] 'There should be a steady stream of
keen, well-trained congregational singers coming out from
schools to take their part in the common worship of the
church.'[48] Not only is no allowance made for the difference
in principle and in atmosphere between the state and the
church school, it would not be claiming too much to say that
this book proceeds on the view that the Act turned the state
schools into church schools. The problem of inter-
denominational instruction having been solved, no further
hindrance remained. The substance, as the Bishop said,
remains the same.

Since with the late forties and the fifties we are dealing
with the tradition of school worship which, although now
very careworn, continues to influence practice today, it is
worth our while to consider some of its characteristics. The
most consistent advice offered by the worship manuals is that
the key to worship is atmosphere and the key to atmosphere
is preparation. 'The hall is the most beautiful room in the
school. Furniture is of the minimum, and the walls are hung
with a series of pictures all showing powerfully the openness
and virility of life out of doors. The space behind a terracotta
jug on the cupboard at the end throws into clear relief
branches of young beech leaves; the polished surface of the
big table reflects golden masses of long stalked buttercups. As
they wait the children see all this; it is a place fit for the
worship of God.'[49] 'The platform should be arranged
differently for worship than at other times; there might be a
table with a coloured cloth, a Cross, carefully arranged
flowers; the Bible placed prominently on a reading desk, and
a good picture of some religious subject changed from time
to time . . . a text or short quotation which summarizes the
theme of the service and is labelled "Thought for the Day"

could be clearly displayed. . .'[50]

There is no doubt at all that the school assembly was understood to be worship in the full sense of the word. This is seen most clearly in a work by C.L. Berry in 1946, the first book which sought to interpret to the schools the exact meaning of those parts of the Act which dealt with the school assembly. 'Religious worship, in secondary schools, as everywhere else, must be nothing less than the rendering unto Almighty God of the honour, the veneration and — most perfect of all worship — the adoration which is due to Him as Creator and Redeemer, and the Love which is due to Him as Himself Eternal Love.'[51] This definition of worship is adhered to very strictly. Even a theme of worship, such as some particular virtue or moral lesson, is avoided since the sole purpose of worship is praise. Confession and intercession are rejected, for worship is what we offer, not what we ask or receive. Although the Act does not specify that the worship shall be Christian, Berry interprets the intention of the Act correctly in remarking ' . . . certainly all schools established by Local Education Authorities are undenominational . . . and are not anti-denominational . . . their pupils are drawn from many denominations of Christianity, with perhaps a small minority of non-Christians'.[52] The height of rigour is reached in the observation that according to the Act 'the worship must be "on the part of" and not merely "in the name of or on behalf of" all pupils in attendance at the school'.[53] Immense care is given (and this also is a typical feature of the period in question) not to offend denominational feeling but in this book, typical of many, there is little sign of interest in the effect of the worship on the children. Since worship is of value in itself, its effect on the worshipper is a matter of relative indifference.

Although they are not pressed with such extraordinary rigour the booklet by H.T. Salzer exhibits the same beliefs. ' . . . in worship we try to draw near to God, to be with Him, serve Him, make offering to Him'.[54] School assembly will consist of such worship and of nothing else, 'so that all come to realize that school prayers are only part of a powerful stream of "this world" and "other worldly" activity and service "with angels and archangels and with all the company of heaven . . ." in which it is their glorious duty and privilege to take part'.[55] The emphasis in worship is upon the inward, the mystical, the spiritual, the contemplative concentration upon the angelic world.

The strengths of the school assembly of this period are seen most clearly in books by Miss J.M. Ferguson and Doris Starmer Smith.[56] It is recognized that the normal type of liturgical service is often inadequate for the day school, and that many traditional prayers are too abstract and insufficiently related to the experience of ordinary young people. Extra biblical readings are included, not only from the religious and theological classics and from modern Christian authors but from the Koran, and Zendavesta and from Hindu sources. Child participation is emphasized, some of the services being actually planned by children. Suggestions are made about the use of recorded music. The extracts and the litanies are often beautiful and it was a great pity that later books, such as those by Berry and the Oxford Diocese, felt unable to follow this example of liberty but plunged children back into an unbending formal liturgy.

But (and some of these criticisms apply to the books by Starmer Smith and Ferguson as well as being generally true throughout the forties and fifties) one is often surprised to find how introverted these assembly books are. Prayers for Animals, Armed Forces and Armistice Day may be found, often conveniently arranged in alphabetical order, and intercession regarding Commonwealth and Country, Government and Girl Guides may sometimes follow, but apart from this sort of thing, couched often in the most theological and metaphysical language, there is little concern with the problems of the world. The Christian virtues, especially those presumed to be most needed by schoolboys (honesty, punctuality, purity and diligence) are earnestly sought on their behalf by ever hopeful teachers; the church year is dutifully celebrated, prefects are duly installed and members of staff from time to time die; the term begins and after a while it ends. It is a cosy, orderly, rather trivial little world.[57]

There is all too little about the great issues of the world in which these young people are growing up. There is little attempt to offer to God the needs of the homeless, the victims of oppression and disaster, the destitute and the aged.

The sick, a more traditional object for Christian charity, are well catered for. But there is almost no attempt to include entertainment and leisure within the world of God. All too often there is an astonishing superficiality in dealing with human relationships. Even in Miss Ferguson's book, which as we have seen, is one of the better books, more sensitive and more imaginative than most, the nearest approach to a secular comment is an extract from one of Emerson's essays on friendship, a quotation from Plato's *Phaedra* on the family and one from L.P. Jacks on facing difficulties. A couple of other extracts are psychological or moralistic in content — Emerson on self-reliance, Carlyle on the use of time — but everything else is religious in the devotional and theological senses. Of God's concern for the secular world there is hardly a trace. Of money, class, colour, war, there is no evidence. But the Gregorian Sacramentary is there, so is St Chrysostom and St Augustine.

Implicit is the assumption that all that matters is the relationship between the soul and God; the movement of thought is too often upward, too seldom outward. Morning Assembly seldom faced the world; it usually retreated into an artificially constructed world of religion which hung suspended over the life of the school.

Associated with these features is the attitude of many of the school worship books of that period towards nature. Here we find a treasury of poetry and prayer expressing the cosmological and teleological arguments for the existence of God, sometimes becoming a veritable nature mysticism and even expressing a frank pantheism.[58] Anyone, the compilers seem to be saying, can see there is a God if he looks hard enough. But he must look at the natural world, not at the world of human relationships, and even then he must usually look not in nature but through nature and beyond it.

Too often the pages of the school worship books of the forties and fifties are marred by a sentimental and naive approach to life. A book for the eleven to fifteen age range contains the following rich examples: 'Go, pretty child and bear this flower unto thy little Saviour'; 'Let thy praise go up as birds go up, that when they wake shake off the dew and soar'; 'O little lark, you need not fly to seek your master in the sky', and Tennyson's 'O mother, how can ye keep me tethered to you — shame'. This last line cannot but sound amusing to modern youth. The poetry selected for the anthologies seems to be particularly prone to this sickly lyricism, over-reaching itself in the effort to be pure and ennobling. The books produced by D.M. Prescott[59] are helpful, with a great deal of useful material and, consistent with the view of the Moral Rearmament Movement which they represent, strike a note of untroubled idealism and confidence. The Four Absolutes of honesty, purity, unselfishness and love are expressed in stories telling of the guidance of God in difficult situations, how God's message was written down and how the change in one man changed a nation. This simple evangelical MRA piety was fully consistent with the prevailing spirituality of assembly in the fifties. Such books were seldom tough enough about the ugliness and pain of the world.[60]

A few other observations on the place of school worship in the Agreed Syllabuses of this period may be of interest. The fundamental influence, as already stated, is that of Cambridgeshire 1939. Sometimes the whole of the Cambridgeshire article 'Religion and Corporate Life in the School' is reprinted, as for example in Bristol 1946, but usually only the part of the article headed 'Corporate Prayer' and beginning 'The centre and focus of such a corporate ideal will naturally be the time when the school comes together for prayer' is used.[61] This was, for example, reprinted in the influential Sunderland Syllabus of 1944 under the heading 'School Worship' and subsequent acknowledgement is often made to both Cambridgeshire and Sunderland when the article is reprinted.[62] Sometimes the Cambridgeshire article on 'Religion and Corporate Life in the School' is split, the first part being modified to become an opening article and the latter part (under the influence of Sunderland) becoming an appendix on 'School Worship';[63] sometimes only the first part is used in modified form;[64] sometimes it is only the second part, abridged, which appears.[65]

Another influence upon the Agreed Syllabuses was the article on worship in *The Background to the Agreed Syllabus*[66] of the Westmorland Education Authority which won fame through being used (together with the Cambridgeshire material) in the 1947 West Riding Syllabus. The resulting article was often reprinted from West Riding.[67]

The West Riding Syllabus had already achieved acclaim in its 1937 edition and an interesting example of the way the syllabuses were composed is the history of the sentence about assembly from this 1937 edition which reads: 'It should not be merely an opening ceremony but rather a preparation for the day, the influence of which will be felt throughout the day.'[68] This sentence was taken over by the Westmorland *Background to the Agreed Syllabus* and found its way back into the West Riding Syllabus in 1947 with the quotation marks from Westmorland still surrounding it. Meanwhile, the sentence had already been quoted in Cambridgeshire 1939, presumably direct from its original West Riding source, although no reference is provided. The 1949 Cambridgeshire Syllabus incorporates the sentence directly into its text[69] presumably because the reasons for the sentence appearing in quotation marks in the 1939 edition were not understood, but also because by then the sentence had become part of the stock in trade of the Agreed Syllabus makers. The history of this little sentence could be repeated with many other similar statements, which seemed to strike a chord of response and were used and adapted freely. Constructing an article on school worship had become rather like making a gospel. The sayings which circulated were inserted in any context where they seemed apt.

A small number of syllabuses provided independent articles on school worship, although most should really be described as only semi-independent since they are similar in general outline and often in details of expression to those we have been discussing. London 1947 has a six-page article. It is emphasized that the worship must express and grow out of 'an environment in which the child may acquire the elementary virtues unconsciously. The Christian ideal of conduct should permeate its life . . .'[70] With regard to the sixth form, we are advised that 'the morning assembly can help to direct the critical faculty to constructive ends by introducing the child (sic) to ideas which are ahead of his psychological needs, so that he is given room for spiritual growth and made aware of a body of critical scholarship which is consistent with faith.'[71] It is fairly normal in literature of this kind that the critical faculties are lead into areas consistent with faith and that the growth pattern of the adolescent is thought to follow the lead offered by the expression 'spiritual growth' by which Christian belief and character is intended.

The York 1948 Syllabus sees worship becoming more of a formal affirmation of faith, as the work of the earlier years comes to fruition in loyalty to the spiritual bonds of the school community. Worship will then be 'a solemn proclamation'.[72] The end result of school worship is that it should 'dispose the children to a habit of worship which will remain with them throughout life'.[73]

Norwich 1951 opens with an article on 'Worship and the School' which emphasizes that because a large number of children will have no contact with religion except through the school it is all the more important that it should 'spring from a living belief and devotion'. A number of simple and helpful suggestions are made as to how this might be effected. This is one of the earliest comments on the increasing problem facing the schools in the secularization of their pupils.

Hertfordshire 1954 contains a clearly set out statement of six pages on the subject 'School Worship'. Worship is related to a native capacity for wonder which is expressed through hero worship and ultimately in adoration of God. The aspects of prayer are described by reference to the Lord's Prayer. The school will be taught that 'all religious instruction is part of the preparation for school worship',[74] and as the children grow older and as the worship is supported by lessons dealing with its various aspects, so finally 'All classroom preparation and the general ordering of the school should culminate in the act of worship, and, when the Assembly Hall is being used as a church, the atmosphere of reverence is vital.'

One of the more unusual essays is found in Lancashire 1948. It is a historical and theological study of the origins, nature and significance of worship. It is unusual in that it is simply called 'Worship' and there is no reference whatever to the school or to young people.[75]

Finally, mention should be made of the considerable number of syllabuses which make little or no reference to worship. Some, like Lindsey 1951, simply have a note drawing the attention of the schools to the requirement of

the Act and adding a few sentences of comment.[76] Others do
not offer a separate article on the subject but include a good
deal of treatment of worship in the syllabus content. Surrey
1945 falls into this category, most sections of the syllabus
being divided into two parts, the second of which is 'The
Christian Life' and nearly always includes consideration of
worship. The Exeter Syllabus of 1945 adopts a similar
pattern dividing each section into belief, worship, conduct
and fellowship. Other examples of this approach are Bootle
(1946), Barrow-in-Furness (1946) and Portsmouth (1952)
which, by the way, is an unusually handsome and attractively
printed book.

We are left with an interesting group of syllabuses which
are strangely silent about worship. The Plymouth Syllabus of
1946 makes virtually no reference to the subject apart from a
few words in the syllabus for the fifteen plus age group.
Cornwall 1946 is similar. There are short paragraphs on
'hymns' and 'prayers' and a short supplementary course for
seniors on prayer. This syllabus is in effect that of York 1930
with a supplement added in 1946 when it was adopted in
Cornwall. Other examples are the Derbyshire Syllabus for
pupils over fifteen years of age (1947) and the Birmingham
Syllabus of 1952 which is dependent upon Smethwick 1947.
The latter has some references to the Festivals of the
Christian year. The Welsh Syllabus of 1945, which although
not an officially agreed syllabus was used by fourteen out of
the seventeen Welsh authorities,[77] has almost no reference to
worship apart from mentioning it in connection with the
teaching of Jesus and the life of the early Christian church.

It is difficult to suggest reasons for this absence of special
treatment for·worship in this group of syllabuses. Since they
also largely ignore the ideas about the Christian values of the
school (although sometimes this seems taken for granted) it
may be that they represent a layer of syllabus tradition older
than the Cambridgeshire Syllabus of 1924. The fact that
many of them are very short, and that often they concentrate
on biblical passages in the old manner supports this. It is
remarkable that York 1930 found Authorities even after
1944 willing simply to adopt it. It may also be that in areas
where non-conformist and High Church Anglican polarization
was acute, the committees might tend to avoid worship,

which might have given rise to denominational controversy. This could have been the case in Wales and Cornwall, although it is difficult to explain the situation in the West Midlands in these terms.

In the sixties school worship began to change. The changes were long overdue. In a number of service books the Authorized Version of the Bible was at last sunk without trace and here and there the use of the modern pronoun when addressing God began to creep in.[78] But it is in the City of Oxford *Handbook on Religious Education*[79] that something really significant almost breaks through. The chapter on worship[80] begins in a startling way. Worship is considered against the background of twentieth-century secularism on a global scale. Communism, materialism and aspects of the impact of science are described as destroying worship. Then Dietrich Bonhoeffer, described as 'a Christian prophet of our time', is introduced asking his famous question about the possibility of prayer and worship in a time of no religion at all. We are then told, 'Bonhoeffer's question cannot be avoided by anyone responsible for the care and nurture of children.' But then, just as we seem on the point of some adventurous thinking about the role of worship in school today, the tone changes and in the rest of the opening section we are back considering the time-honoured problems of making school worship relevant and how to encourage a child to join a church when he leaves school. There follow[81] three outline courses for classroom use intended to teach children about Christian worship. These sections are good, and here we find at last an attempt to place worship into a context of education. The producers of the Oxford Handbook were evidently in a dilemma. How could Bonhoeffer's question be answered without making recommendations which might be contrary to the Act?[82]

2 Worship and Education: Some Distinctions

We have seen that school worship in England and Wales expresses a fairly consistent understanding of the nature of worship. There was a certain development up to about 1939 but there does not seem to have been much change since then. In very recent years methods have changed considerably but the concept of worship in school has not changed much.

The ideas about worship which circulated in the schools were not particularly distinctive of the school. We have seen that there was little attempt to adapt the concept of worship for the state school, although there was some truncation because of the non-sacramental nature of school worship and there was a growing concern that it should be comprehensible and enjoyable to children. Nevertheless, the ideas about worship which we found in the schools are broadly the same as those which were current about worship in the churches.

It may be helpful to summarize these ideas. Some of this may perhaps be rather commonplace, but we will emphasize those aspects which will become important at a later stage of our enquiry.

Worship in the history and literature of school assembly is understood as *an explicit, direct and appropriate response to God who has the right to the total loyalty of the believer.*

Let us look in detail at this definition.

Worship is that attitude which confers supreme worth upon the admired object of its attention. It evaluates the object of its activity as being utterly worthy.[1]

Worship understood literally is that attitude towards God expressed in so many words (or actions). Its response to God is direct; he is explicitly addressed as God. There are various uses of the word worship which have an attenuated or metaphorical significance which we will consider in a few moments. In these secondary senses the attitudes or beliefs or commitments expressed in worship are given a less articulate form. They are no less important in the life of the Christian but because they are indirect they should not be described as literal worship.

Worship is appropriate in so far as it is adapted to the nature of the worshipped object. This adaptation is part of the consequence of perceiving supreme worth in God. That which is confessed as supremely valuable must control the form of the worship and the life of the worshipper. So a peaceful deity is worshipped implicitly by the pursuit of peace and explicitly by words and actions directed towards him and affirming and adoring his nature as peaceful. A holy deity is worshipped implicitly by a holy life and directly and overtly by adoring him for his holiness. It is easy to see that without the support of a holy life, the worship of God in its direct and literal form alone is insufficient and even hypocritical. The life as lived must be appropriate to the worship as offered, as the Hebrew prophets declared. Nevertheless, it is useful to distinguish between the literal worship of liturgy and cult and the ethical consequences of this worship. But in both cases, the value placed upon the worshipful attributes of God would be less than absolute unless the response was adapted to his worshipped nature. This is the reason why it is an essential part of worship that it should be appropriate.

Worship is a response. This means that it is active. It may take the form of words, actions, thoughts and attitudes. The *intention* to respond in this particular worshipful way is the central feature. Yet, in spite of its deliberateness as activity, worship remains a reply, a response.[2] It is evoked by the conception of the deity who in Christian thought always retains the initiative. One is summoned to worship and called to prayer.

The response is directed towards something or other. The verb 'to worship' is a transitive verb. One does not simply worship, or worship nothing; one worships God or a surrogate. This follows from the nature of worship as response and as the conferring of supreme value upon the divine caller. From the point of view of the worshipper, the value is not so much conferred as recognized; it is already there. Worship can be offered to an unknown God (although it would be difficult to know what would be appropriate) but worship cannot be offered to nothing at all.

Christian worship thus logically entails certain beliefs. We can express this by saying that it has a cognitive content and these cognitions are re-cognized. If someone worships God, his worship not only implies but logically requires that he should believe that there is a God and that his nature is such as to command worship.[3] During times of discussion and reflection, these beliefs may be held up for criticism or may even be suspended. But during worship the beliefs must be assumed, otherwise the adoring commitment which is the heart of worship will be impaired. Regardless of the stage of clarification which theological reflection has achieved, worship always takes place on the far side of that kind of critical and self-conscious reflection. Worship need not be theologically naive, but however informed by theology it may be, the essential difference between theologizing and worshipping lies in the relationship between the subject and his cognitions at the time of his activity.

The object of worship is thought of as possessing rights over the worshipper. This must be the case since worship is a response not to a mere fellow human being nor to nature thought of as natural but to the divine. That which is thought of as divine exercises a certain kind of constraint over man. If any object, whether human or otherwise, is conceived of as wielding by right of its nature this kind of powerful demand, it has to that extent been deified. The demand of God wins the consent of the believer who thus considers it his duty and his joy to offer worship.

Worship may be distinguished from respect and admiration by its totality. The demand of God is felt as absolute. He represents not only worth but supreme worth. In so far as his goodness, his love and his power are absolute and infinite, so the worship appropriately offered to him is unconditional.

This totality of demand requires the allegiance of the worshipper. God is worshipped as Lord. Because of this totality and the beliefs involved it is both logically and psychologically impossible to offer worship to conflicting images of deity. It is the very nature of worship which prohibits the adoration of both God and Mammon. Supreme worth cannot be conferred upon both for each denies a part of the other. If God and Mammon converge, to that degree, worship of both becomes possible. But if they conflict, the man who worships both must experience severe cognitive dissonance. The most common way of reducing this dissonance and enabling men of different faiths to worship together is to reduce the absolute nature of worship. But when this is done, it is either no longer an appropriate response to the God of Christianity, or else God himself must be denied the absolute perfections which the Christian tradition has ascribed to him. The future of Christian worship and the future of Christian faith in the transcendent perfections of God are one and indivisible.

This, then, is the attitude towards worship which we see in the schools during the period of our survey. It is a thoroughly sensible, normal and orthodox attitude. The schools are to be criticized, however, for failing to give sufficient consideration to the relationship between worship and education. But before we turn to this subject, let us look at some of the aspects of worship, particularly those which are important in introducing it to children and young people.

Worship may be thought of as affirmation. It is saying 'yes' to God and as such has its roots in saying 'yes' to creation. Worship when offered to the Lord and Giver of life must be life-affirming. In saying 'yes' to life the child enters upon the threshold of worship. In literal worship the attributes of God are affirmed as being perfect, worthy, desirable and admirable. In prayer this is expressed in invocation, in which God is addressed through a list of epithets: 'Oh most holy and loving God, all wise and all powerful . . .' But for those too young to appreciate this, the attitude of affirmation to all which God is worshipped for making might be a more appropriate response. For the response of worship must be appropriate not only to the object of adoration but also to the degree of belief and understanding of the worshipper. Otherwise it may lose its truthful and sincere intention. If a child cannot affirm the beauty and truth of religious beliefs because he cannot understand them (and it is for the psychologist to decide whether we may believe that he can or cannot), then when something is arranged especially for him, the child should be encouraged to affirm the beauty and truth of what lies within his experience. The capacity for worship waits upon the development of the entailed cognitions. To put it baldly, worship arises out of what you feel about your beliefs. No beliefs, no feelings about them, then no worship. But if a child is helped to affirm joyfully what lies within his reach, at least the intention of worship to affirm beauty and truth joyfully is retained. Cognitive enrichment will follow as the child matures emotionally and his grasp of religious language increases. In this way the experience of the child can form part of a ladder leading through increased belief and deepened feeling to worship which can intend to be literal worship of God.

We have already spoken of adults suspending their doubts and their questionings in order to worship with committed adoration. Why is it better that children incapable of faith in the doctrines should be encouraged to express some attitude preliminary to worship which does not require affirmation of the doctrine, but adults whose faith in the doctrines is wavering may be encouraged to suspend their disbelief from time to time in order to worship? Does not the worship of those adults lose its truth and integrity?

If a child is incapable of understanding the beliefs upon which worship rests, he is incapable of hypocrisy. He cannot affirm nor deny, nor can he pretend to affirm or deny. There is no reason why he should not be taken with his parents while they worship, and since we will see as our discussion proceeds that nurture by the church is a perfectly legitimate activity, there is no reason why the church should not hope and expect that although its own young children will not be able to worship during the adult services, they may nevertheless be enriched with a variety of ancillary experiences which will prove to have been a preparation for worship when they are older. In the meantime the church offers its worship to God on behalf of its baptized children. But when a ceremony of some kind is being arranged especially for children, then it is better for it to be within their grasp, even if this means (as it must in the case of young children) that the resulting service will not necessarily be worship since the doctrines will not be affirmed. It will be a different form of preparation for later worship. The difference will lie in the fact that in the adult service they are present during worship but in their own service a threshold is deliberately being constructed for them. In the case of children in the state school the situation is different again, since it is no part of the business of the state school to religiously nurture its pupils.

Adults are, of course, capable both of affirmation and of hypocrisy. If a person's doubts have reached the point where Christian faith no longer represents the general orientation of his life and he no longer has any intention of living according to it, it would certainly be insincere for him to worship. Theological enquiry itself, however, does not imply doubt but simply a readiness to think. Theology implies being open to the possibility of doubt and of imagining what it is like to doubt, but the theologian when he worships no longer enquires but rejoices, gives thanks and adores. The object of his enquiry and the adoration both express the direction of his life. The move from enquiry to worship and back again is therefore harmonious. Between these two examples (the man who has given up his faith and the one who enquires into his faith) there will be every possible shade of variety, and only the individual can know when his worship (or his lack of worship) no longer represents the main intention of his life. There will, however, be many cases where a person who is in general a believer may nevertheless have serious and gnawing doubts about some aspect of the faith to which he is committed. Such a person may in good conscience suspend his doubts when he worships although he may not use worship to evade permanently the force of his doubts. On the other hand there will be some whose doubts arise from factors of an emotional or an interpersonal kind; such people may hope that in worship their particular kind of doubts will be resolved and there is nothing about this hope which lacks integrity or sincerity. 'Lord, I believe; help me in my unbelief' can be a perfectly proper act of worship for believers in these situations.

Related to the affirmation of life is the celebration of life. One not only says 'yes'; one shouts 'hurrah!' Celebration is the ritual dignification of the peak experiences of life. In worship these great turning points and crises (the ending of the year, sickness, birth, marriage, death, coming of age and so on) are recognized in a group activity which enables their significance to be grasped and at the same time deepened by relating that particular experience to all the others of the sequence, thus holding life together in a dramatically coherent frame. It is typical of Christian worship that it celebrates not only the happy events but the solemn and even the tragic. By celebrating it, death is redeemed from its most offensive feature, namely, its triviality. A celebration of death speaks to death in the name of the conscious life which moves always towards it. The status of death is decided in its relation to those who celebrate it.

Worship as celebration has its roots in a culture which is rich in celebration of all kinds. But if the society is celebration starved, if the people do not remember the great events of their past, if there is little festivity and ceremony, then this aspect of worship will often lose its power. As with affirmation, to those for whom the theological beliefs assumed by worship are too difficult, the way of celebration offers a beginning. In celebrating birthdays, the seasons, the victory of sporting teams, partings and home-comings, Guy Fawkes Day, St Valentine's Day and April Fool's Day, children are introduced to custom, repetition, ritual commemorations and all the outlook upon life which sees it as worthy of shouting 'hurrah!' The use of parades and processions, of songs and clapping and the significance attached to fire, to eating, to kissing and so on all play a part in preparing in the child an attitude which may some day be enriched by mature faith.

Ultimate concern is another characteristic aspect of worship. The worship expresses what the believer regards as being of final importance, that which is taken seriously without any reservations. This has its roots in the important concerns of the rest of our lives and worship becomes insincere when the concern which it expresses is no longer the finally serious concern of the worshipper. When children can be encouraged to express the concern suitable to their age and interests and to discriminate between the selfish and the unselfish concern, the trivial and temporary and the permanent and important concern, they are beginning to develop the attitudes typical of worship although not exclusive to it.

Self re-orientation is a characteristic intention of worship.

The worshipper seeks to bring his life, his aspirations, his values and his ambitions into harmony with the beliefs he affirms in worship. In worship he redirects himself or realigns himself with the divine life: 'Thy will be done on earth as it is in heaven'. It is while worshipping that the believer realizes again that his heart is not pure nor his hands clean, as he asks 'Who shall ascend unto the hill of the Lord and who shall stand in his holy place?' So we find that penitence is often the first stage of worship and rededication its climax. As he hears the call to worship the believer realizes the gulf between him and God. 'Be holy, for I am holy.'

Communion with God is another aspect of worship. The worshipper seeks to participate in the divine life. The eucharistic feast, where the worshippers share the body and blood of the Lord, is the clearest example of this aspiration in Christian worship. For a threshold of readiness for this, we must look to everything which relates man intimately to the other, whether the otherness of persons or of nature. Ultimately, the aspiration in worship to overcome the gulf of separation has its origin in the union of mother and child, a union which is lost with maturity, but glimpsed again in the ecstatic adoration of sexual union and religious communion.

Adoration is the last aspect of worship we shall consider. The capacity to adore the other is no doubt also generated during early infancy, but in worship it is particularly significant for while the other aspects of worship express to some extent attitudes towards the self, other people and the world, adoration defines the relationship towards God only. It expresses directly that personal relationship of unqualified admiration and trustful praise which is central to the act and attitude of Christian worship.

Affirmation, celebration, the expression of ultimate concern, self-reorientation, communion and adoration: these are the aspects or characteristics of worship with which we shall be especially concerned. They are the paths through which the churches may attempt to build a readiness for worship in young people and they will provide a means whereby the Christian and the religious educator can interpret as relevant to worship the secularized and deliberately ambiguous state school assemblies which we will be considering in chapter 6. At that point of our discussion we will return to these aspects of worship.

In recent years there has been a tendency to describe as worship any activity or attitude which has some affinity with worship. It has proved possible in this way to disguise the nature of the changes which are taking place in the way school worship is sometimes conducted. Because worship of the Christian creator God involves reverence for all life, some teachers have been claiming as worship any act or statement which embodies this attitude. Reverence for life is, however, merely a necessary ingredient for a definition of worship; it must be there, but it is not sufficient. We have tried to distinguish between worship and other related activities by using the expression 'threshold of worship' for the activities which have something important in common with worship.

In addition to the notion of 'threshold' which suggests entrance into, continuity with, and preparation for worship, it might be useful to offer the expression 'secular worship' as a rather paradoxical description for the activities which although significantly related to worship also lack some of the attributes of literal worship.

'Secular worship' might be used to describe four kinds of activities. In the first place secular worship may be worship the object of which is not an alleged transcendent reality but a mundane one. It is possible in this sense to worship sport or one's spouse. Such worship may have all the psychological features of literal religious worship but since a transcendent reference is lacking it is correctly described as being secular, appertaining to this world and this age alone. To the Christian, such secular worship must appear blasphemous since that which is not ultimately worthy of such adoration is treated as if it were.

Secondly, secular worship may be used to describe worship which although directed towards a transcendent reality is not expressed within a religious community. It is non-church worship but not non-God worship. It retains, however, the intention of worship. A believer may pray while walking to work. Since it is consciously directed towards God this type of worship is still literally worship.

There is a third sense which 'secular worship' may have. We may speak of worshipping God not only in the midst of but through our daily work or through our appreciation of art and music. Here we are concerned with activities which although not carried out whilst thinking of God are dedicated to his glory. The religious believer would regard this use of the word 'worship' as legitimate.[4] Indeed, we have already seen that literal worship cannot be valid unless it is accompanied by this kind of secular worship. In the first sense of 'secular worship' it was the object of worship which was secular; in the second and third senses it is merely the manner. But while the second use of 'secular worship' still retains a literal sense of worship, in this third sense 'worship' is used metaphorically. It is not the explicit articulation of adoration of God but an ethical consequence of sincere worship.

'Secular worship' may finally be used to indicate an attitude which shares certain characteristics with literal religious worship but which is not directed towards any reality, transcendent or mundane, overtly or by implication. The verb 'to worship' is here used in an intransitive sense. It consists in the cultivation and the expression of certain attitudes and habits of mind such as reverence, trustfulness, joy, or a meditative attitude towards life. Worship is here removed from its theological cognitions and we are left with the psychological affinities. These affinities are important in themselves and in the development of the capacity to worship a religious object, but since such an object is neither denied nor intended nor held in mind, the religious believer would regard this final type of secular worship as a legitimate activity but (like the third sense) a metaphorical use of the word 'worship'.

The expression 'pre-worship' may serve as a synonym for 'threshold of worship'. Anything in the history of an individual, or a family, or in the policies of a church or a school which helps to develop capacities without which worship would be unlikely to appear may be described as 'pre-worship'. The development of such capacities may provide a programme for nurture into worship, and the various senses of 'secular worship' if worked into programmes of this sort may become examples of threshold or pre-worship.

We turn now to consider the nature of education. We can distinguish a general process of education from a specific process. The general process is that entire relationship between the generations in which the total culture of a society is passed on and renewed. In this broadest sense, everything we are which has not been genetically inherited, our language, our outlook, all that has been learned, is the product of education.

This general sense of education can be broken down into a number of specific activities. These include socialization, training, instruction, indoctrination, evangelization, catechesis, nurture, schooling and education in the specific sense. We will describe the main characteristics of these various specific processes in order to highlight the distinctive features of specific education and in order to see that worship has different relationships with different processes.

The essence of training is that skills are taught and acquired without any necessary accompanying knowledge of the principles upon which an understanding of the skills depends. The skills involved in training are usually physical manipulations and usually have to be carried out in an invariable order. You can be trained to drive a car, to type or to dance. Repetition of the sequence of manipulations is the main method of training. The trained person can be as efficient in his task as the person who is also educated in the principles of the task. Looking at two cars being driven, you could not tell which driver was trained and which was also educated. But the trained driver is less flexible. He can only offer a limited application of his expertise and when the car breaks down, he is reduced to trial and error. It is important to notice that for the performance of certain tasks, training is much more efficient than education. A person may be educated in the principles of motor mechanics but be unable to drive a car. He may be blind, or he may simply never have learned. You cannot drive a car unless you are trained and you cannot mend a car unless you are educated. On the other hand, although there is an important and legitimate role for training, it is important to notice that while we train animals, we do not educate them. Education is for people only.

The role of training in the religious sphere is rather limited, but it is possible to train children to repeat the words of prayers and to sing hymns, to look up passages in the Bible and to reply in correct adult language to religious questions.[5]

Indeed, in so far as a habit is a repeated sequence of gestures or motions, what are called good habits, whether in religion or in morals, are perhaps acquired through training, although if they continue to be performed for no other reason than trained habit, we could not properly describe them as being either good or religious.

In instruction the emphasis is on the verbal content rather than upon the physical manipulations. Instruction is what you tell someone when you are training him. Not all training implies instruction; you might train a deaf man by showing him. In showing, he learns by imitation; in instruction he learns by obedience. The difference between training and showing is, however, rather tenuous, since you might be said to be instructing through your gestures and the learner might be said to obediently imitate you. But that there is a difference can be seen from the fact that although we learn by imitating ourselves (e.g. the baby who learns to speak partly through listening to himself and repeating the sounds he hears himself making) we find it odd to speak of instructing ourselves. Instruction, unlike imitation, requires a source of authority other than ourselves. We may therefore be trained by imitation or by instruction and the latter involves verbal direction from another. Similarly, not all instruction implies training. You may instruct some one in the principles of astronomy without training him to actually do anything. But he would need training to use a telescope skilfully. You may instruct a person in an ideology and this may not involve any training. But although training and instructing do not always coincide, they have in common the fact that they are usually orderly and sequential. It is precisely because instruction is orderly and sequential that it is a more efficient way of training a person to drive a car than simply letting him drive round a stadium discovering for himself what he has to do. The orderly and sequential nature of instruction indicates its confidence and its authority. Instruction is always authoritative and usually delivered in an authoritative manner. The army officer instructs the recruit in the use of the field gun. 'First we have the naming of parts . . .' Instruction is usually supported by a manual, a directory, a handbook, in which the agreed authoritative content is set out in an orderly manner.

Instruction is an important form of communication for
Christian faith. The importance of an agreed manual in order
to guarantee the authority of the instruction finds classical
expression in the Agreed Syllabus of Religious Instruction.
The agreement is to exlude controversial areas and thus make
it possible to instruct in the remainder.[6] The principle of
exclusion of controversial areas is, of course, older than the
Agreed Syllabuses, going back, as we have seen, to the
Cowper-Temple clause of the Forster Education Act 1870.
But while the exclusion of distinctive denominational teaching made proselytizing impossible, the emergence of positive
agreement in the 1920s and 1930s made instruction possible.
Thus the neutrality of the period following 1870 gives way to
the vigorous instruction of the period following 1944.[7]
Without agreement, one cannot instruct; one can only have a
discussion. Discussion is contrary to the spirit of instruction,
which is why, when instruction was beginning to disappear in
the early 1960s, there was such interest in the so-called
'discussion methods'.[8]

Why is it that similarities between religious or denominations are so important to instruction? Agreed Syllabuses
were really lists of similarities between denominations. This is
partly because the list of similarities defines the area to be
covered, and since instruction (unlike specific education) is
content centred, definition of area to be covered is vital to it.
But there is more to it than this. After all, a list of
dis-similarities could equally exactly define an area to be
covered. But to instruction, it matters that the area to be
covered should consist of similarities, not dis-similarities. This
is because the controversial cannot be presumed to be true.
Any breath of controversy, therefore, between parts of the
content of the area to be covered weakens the authority of
all the content. You could still, of course, instruct about the
dis-similarities, as an officer might instruct his men about the
differences between two types of gun, but religious instruction is interested in instructing in the truth.

In order to make it possible for them to instruct in the
truth (although, in the opinion of any one of them, not the
full truth) the churches involved in Agreed Syllabuses passed
over the features which made them distinctive. It is true that
the possibility of choice is lessened when the distinctions

between options are not clarified. Instruction, however, is not much interested in the facilitation of intelligent choice by showing what there is to choose between; it proceeds on the assumption that the choice has been made or that the only choice is to be for the instruction or against it. That there might be various instructions is a possibility with which instruction cannot deal.[9]

There is, of course, a proper place for instruction just as there is for training. When learning to use a mortar, you cannot be experimenting with novel ideas of your own about what would happen if you did this or that instead of what the instruction manual or the instructor himself tells you. Instruction is safe and responsible. Similarly, it is perfectly proper for religious and political groups to offer instruction in their respective tenets. A disciple may quite properly go to India to be instructed in the doctrines of a Hindu teacher and a candidate for adult Christian baptism may be instructed in the teaching of the Baptist church on that subject. There is nothing degrading or inferior about accepting this form of access to the concentrated experience, belief or expertise of a particular group of people, or this way of acquiring a certain skill. But these examples are of adults deciding to accept the instruction from a certain party in the knowledge that they might have decided otherwise and that the instruction they will receive is not the only one available on this subject. When instruction is offered to children in subjects which (unlike the technique of using a mortar) are essentially controversial, the situation is rather different. This is because the adult knows the instruction to be relative to other instructions and he knows that he has freely chosen to receive it. The child knows neither of these things, and if the instructor makes an attempt to hide knowledge of alternatives from him and to deny him choice, there is a danger that instruction may become indoctrination.

The Christian parent is, therefore, in something of a dilemma. On the one hand it is his duty to pass on to his child that which he sincerely believes to be most beautiful and most true. On the other hand he has a duty to his child to let the child become independent and free. The problems faced by the father and mother instructing the child are like those faced by God instructing man: how can sovereign grace elicit a free response?

Instruction may become indoctrination if an attempt is made to conceal from the pupil that there are other instructions. But in modern societies it is hardly possible to conceal from children the relativity of Christian life and faith. The global village has seen to that. It soon becomes all too apparent to children that their own Christian homes are different, and that not everyone goes to church. In early adolescence the problem is not of hiding non-Christian alternatives but of maintaining some credibility for Christian faith. In a pluralist democracy, cognitive minorities[10] cannot successfully go on instructing young people; they must go one way or the other: they must indoctrinate or they must educate.

It is probably best, then, if the churches reverse the usual order. Instead of instructing first, so that children may have a firm basis upon which to meet education, they should first be nurtured, then educated, then (if and when a free choice has been made) instructed. Instruction should follow awareness of alternatives rather than precede it.[11]

In so far as the children of Britain could be considered Christian, and the schools Christian communities, the Christian instruction offered by the Agreed Syllabuses was not in itself, and in the light of its period, an improper activity. We must distinguish between the right of the community to insist that the schools offer Christian instruction and the right of the community to insist that pupils should receive it. This distinction was always recognized in the 'withdrawal' clauses of the various Education Acts.

Things have changed now. The Christian hegemony has been weakened, and even if Britain could be re-established as an entirely Christian country, young people would know that they lived in a pluralistic world. We could still re-introduce religious instruction into the state schools, but we could no longer allow Christian instruction to be the only one. The schools could open their doors to all who wished to offer instruction in whatever faith or creed and children could be allocated to classes either according to their family tradition or by their own free choice. This is in fact the situation in those countries where clergy of various churches come to the schools to give religious instruction to the children of their community.[12] This might not be wrong in principle. But it would be inadequate if that was all the school offered. After all, what are teachers for? What can they offer which instructors cannot offer? What is education?

Indoctrination is a more complex process but it seems to require the presence of three factors. In the first place the content to be communicated must consist of doctrines. This enables us to distinguish indoctrination from socialization which deals with patterns of social behaviour rather than social, political and religious doctrines. Of course, social behaviour may imply social doctrines and the area between socialization and indoctrination will be blurred. Nevertheless, the distinction enables us to draw a line between teaching children to use cutlery not their fingers when eating (socialization) and teaching children to say grace before meals, which could be indoctrination depending on the presence of the remaining two factors.

The second factor involved in indoctrination is that the doctrines must either already be controversial in the surrounding society or the communicator must seek to prevent them becoming controversial. It may be objected that all doctrines are necessarily controversial, but the point is whether the putative indoctrinator knows this and intends to do something (and not just anything) about it. The doctrine of *mana* in the South Sea Islands is controversial in the sense that its status is ambiguous and its exact psychological or even physical significance may be obscure. But was the religious leader or magical practitioner in the area in the early nineteenth century aware of this? On the other hand the inquisition of the seventeenth century may be described as an indoctrinatory agency since it sought to prevent certain doctrines from becoming controversial within the church. It did this in the firm knowledge that the doctrines in question had already become controversial in European theology as a whole since the Reformation. When the catechists of the pre-reformation period carried out their work, it was probably not indoctrination, because the doctrines were not controversial in their own society nor could there be any attempt to prevent them from becoming so, since the catechists themselves never thought for a minute that there were possibilities of genuine and honest disagreement within

the church on fundamental matters. During periods when the
catechists deliberately sought to exclude from their catechizing the questions raised by heretics, then (provided the next
criterion was also present) their catechizing would have
become indoctrinatory.

The third factor which must be present before a process of
communication can be called indoctrination is that the
communicator must attempt to pass on the doctrines in such
a way as to bypass the reason. This criterion enables us to
distinguish indoctrination from the general influence which a
person's ideas may have on others. Such influence may
bypass the reason in the sense that the influenced person may
be swayed by his admiration for the character of his hero
rather than the force of his ideas, but the hero we have in
mind here is not deliberately avoiding the reason and may
not even realize that he is having any influence. We may
safely say that the crux of indoctrination lies in the intent of
the communicator rather than in his actual success or failure,
and it lies thus in his attitude towards the reason and hence
the will of his subjects.

Indoctrination can only be justified by those to whom
acceptance of an alleged truth is more important than the
status of the man who believes. It is not compatible with
Christianity since the truths proclaimed by Christianity
include truths about the status of man. A Christian communicator who in order to enforce his belief that the will is bound
and the reason fallen ignores the reason and deceives the will
is an agent of the fall and not an agent of the salvation of
man. Christians who argue that they should communicate by
indoctrinatory methods because others have no compunction
in doing so are contributing to the corruption they profess to
deplore.

Unlike indoctrination, evangelization seeks to work
through rational means. The evangelist seeks to present a
coherent message which will make an appeal to the mind and
the will of the listener. He hopes to act as the vehicle of the
Word of God to reactivate the will and awaken the dulled
mind. He may try to engage the reason and the will by
stirring the emotions. The Christian arguments against war
may be enlivened by showing a film depicting its horrors. The
film intends to help the imagination to grasp the reasons

given. The question is whether the arousal of the emotions is intended as an aid to the reason or as a substitute for it. If the latter should be the case, we would then accuse the evangelist of using methods more appropriate to the indoctrinator. The evangelist seeks to win the assent of his hearers to his message. The indoctrinator is not interested in assent, which is a rational activity involving judgment and decision, but in conformity in mind and act to his doctrines. Conformity is achieved through wearing down. Assent is achieved through raising up the imagination and the reason and the will.

Preaching is one form of evangelism, but when we consider such things as preaching and teaching, we are talking about very broad methods of communication rather than types of communication involving different principles. Teaching, for example, can be a method of evangelization, or of instruction, or of specific education.

The word nurture can be used in a number of senses and it is perhaps convenient to try to distinguish some of these. In general education, nurture can be used to describe the process of introducing a child to the expectations and habits of society. In this sense nurture might be almost synonymous with socialization, but socialization often centres upon the function of the family and involves the initial uses of language and the capacities for forming human relationships. Nurture can be used not only to cover 'making a child a social being' but to describe the initiation of a child into his culture in a broader sense. The long and ugly word 'enculturization' is sometimes used for this. It has to do with the passing on of existing values and is a conservative function of general education.

Nurture can also be used for the process of helping the self to form itself through its free choices. This would have to do with the increased autonomy and originality of the person, the sort of thing that C.G. Jung meant when he spoke of 'individuation'. We could thus speak of nurturing the inner self. This function of general education would be existential and possibly radical rather than conservative.

Nurture is also used in church education literature where it tends to have the same poles of meaning. It can indicate the role of the tradition, passing on the church's faith and life, or

it can emphasize the nurture of the distinctive selfhood of
the individual Christian.

Nurture is perhaps more commonly used in Protestant
religious general education and catechizing in Catholic
general education.

The processes of nurture and catechesis are like evangelism
in that they intend to present an orderly appeal to the mind
and will. They differ from evangelism because the latter is
normally offered to the unconvinced to win their conviction
but nurture and catechesis are offered to the convinced in
order to deepen their conviction.

Nurture describes the process of bringing a baptized child
of Christian parents to the point where he is ready to endorse
his baptism.[13] The emphasis in nurture is thus upon the
growth of the person and in this respect nurture is more like
specific education. In catechizing the emphasis is more upon
the content and in this way, catechesis is rather like
instruction. On the other hand, catechesis has to do with the
rational unfolding of the contents of a subject matter, and
the link with rationality is an important connection between
catechesis and specific education. It must also be remem-
bered that the concepts of nurture and catechesis have been
subject to mutual influence, and that when catechists today
speak of 'catechesis of experience' they have in mind a building
up of Christian personhood not unlike nurture.[14]

3 *Worship and Education: Some Tensions*

We are now in a position to pick out the main features of the specific education process. As distinct from training, specific education seeks to pass on knowledge of the principles of a subject. This is the difference between a person educated into science and one merely trained into laboratory techniques. If, in being taught some laboratory process, a student is merely shown what manipulations to carry out and in what order, he is being trained only. A historical education means an introduction into the principles of historical events. The act of verbal or written reproduction of the sequence in certain kinds of tests corresponds to the series of manipulations which we saw to be a characteristic feature of training. Since education into a subject implies knowledge of the principles of knowledge (knowing why what is alleged to be known is known, and knowing how to know more) it may be said to consist in the epistemology of the various subjects, i.e. the ways of knowing characteristic of history, science and so on. Whether a subject can be matched with a specific education into that subject depends upon whether it has a distinct epistemological structure. It is appropriate to be trained to use a typewriter and not to be educated to type, since there are no formal epistemological principles of typewriting. If we do speak of the principles of typing we simply mean the rudiments of the techniques, or the generalized rules upon which the instruction is based. These principles do not constitute a way of knowledge. But there are principles of art in a more important sense than the ones we mean when we speak of the principles of using the brush in painting. The latter is simply a rule of practice, but the principles of art which make education into art appropriate to the nature of

art are those which indicate the nature of art as a way of
knowing the world.

The notion of general education may be applied to the
whole of the church's endeavour to pass its life on to
succeeding generations and that will consist of many, perhaps
all, of the processes we have tried to distinguish. There may
be additional processes peculiar to the church's general
education, such as the liturgy. Of course, by including in our
earlier discussion such things as evangelizing, nurture and
catechizing, we have already had the general education
offered by the Christian community in mind. When we come
to specific education, it is clear that specific religious
education can be nothing but whatever specific education is,
only in the field of religion. We notice, in connection with
the point that specific education involves education into the
principles of a subject, that the possibility of religious
specific education depends on whether or not there are forms
of knowing which are distinctive to religion. If there are not,
then we can train, nurture, catechize, instruct and so on, but we
will not be able to specifically education. Religion can make
out a sufficiently strong case, however, for being a distinctive
form of knowing and therefore religious education is a
possibility.

As distinct from instruction, specific education is interested in the person rather than the content. The object of
instruction is to master the content (to 'cover the syllabus');
the object of education is to make mastery of further content
possible and to grasp the principles for the acquisition of that
content. The specific content at any moment in education
serves merely as a vehicle for that purpose. This is why it is
appropriate to have syllabuses of religious instruction.
Specific education into religion will be orderly but that order
will not only consist of a list of materials to be learned or
areas to be covered. Biblical instruction provides a list of
passages or books to be taught. Biblical education is
concerned with hermeneutics.

Of course, hermeneutics is a content also. The content of a
lesson dealing with the principles of biblical interpretation
will be different from the content of a lesson dealing with the
chronology of biblical events or with the memorization of
important biblical passages. The distinction between instruction as being content-based and education as being a person

centred process is therefore not a very clear one. The important feature of the difference between content and process is that education has in mind a more significant type of learning than instruction deals with. What is 'more significant' is to be judged by fundamental beliefs about man, his origin, nature and destiny. When we say that instruction is content centred, we mean that the kind of learning with which instruction is concerned is to do with the acquiring and accepting of a body of knowledge received on authority. Education is to do with the rationality of those facts, with their relevance to the emerging personhood of the pupil, and with their claim to acceptance on grounds of their intrinsic authority, rather than upon the grounds of the guarantee offered by some authority such as the tradition itself. It is obvious that as soon as education concerns itself with questions such as these, the content of an education class will immediately be affected.

Another important difference between specific education and instruction lies in their attitudes towards controversy. We have seen that instruction in religion involved the laying aside by the churches of the features which made them distinctive. But with education, it is the distinctive features which are most important. This is why the Cowper-Temple clause, forbidding denominational distinctiveness, is an impossible basis for education into religion. Because of its critical, exploratory, choice-enhancing nature, specific education highlights the dis-similarities between systems of belief.

How, in the public schools of a pluralistic democracy, are controversial questions to be dealt with? This is one of the basic questions facing education systems in the western world today. It is a question important in the teaching of history, social studies, and even the physical sciences, as well as religion. The alternatives are reasonably clear. The schools could be forbidden to deal with controversial questions at all. This would, however, not only be extremely boring for the schools but it would be a bad preparation for life in a democratic society. Failing this, the schools could teach everything as if it were true and criticize nothing or they could teach nothing as if it were true and criticize everything. The former would be a situation of pluralist instruction. Let us suppose a situation in which each teacher instructs in his own faith. But no teacher ever asks critical questions about any faith. There would be many parallel instructions, for they would never meet. But the best course for the school is the last alternative — to teach nothing as if it was assumed to be true, as if its truth could be taken for granted, and to criticize everything, to expose everything to comparison, to probing, to enquiry.

Specific education is like evangelism and nurturing and unlike indoctrinating in that it seeks to engage the active support of the pupil, to elicit his willing co-operation and to enhance his autonomy. But education differs from these processes in its attitude towards the pupil's attitude towards the content. Evangelization, catechizing and nurturing all seek to win or keep the assent of the pupil. In the case of evangelization, for example, the hearer of the message may go away with a deeper critical awareness of the nature of the message. This would be perfectly consistent with the evangelist's aim, possibly an essential step towards the reaching of his aim, or perhaps a welcome bonus. But the main purpose of the evangelist is to convince his hearer and to secure his commitment. Instruction assumes the assent of the pupil; indoctrination avoids his assent; evangelizing, catechizing and nurturing seek to win, retain and deepen his assent. But education is not concerned with winning the assent of the pupil to the propositions of the content but only to the implications of the method. Education is not mainly concerned with whether the pupils agree that Julius Caesar invaded Britain but with whether they understood the actual methods of finding out, and whether they agree with the importance of finding out rather than simply accepting what text books and traditions say.

Similarly, religious education (unlike religious instruction) is not mainly concerned about whether pupils agree or disagree that Jesus rose from the dead but only in their understanding of what it means religiously that Jesus rose from the dead, or did not. Religious education is thus not concerned with belief or dis-belief but with the grounds for belief and dis-belief.

This means that education must necessarily be deliberately critical of its own content in a way that does not occur to instruction and is deliberately avoided by indoctrination. The example of the resurrection illustrates this criticism of the content. Catechizing and nurturing may be critical of their own content, and these days it is increasingly common to find that this is the case, but they need not be so in order to be themselves. Their tactics may require it but not their nature. If catechism and nurture are self-critical it will be in order to deepen autonomous commitment or to facilitate intelligent assent. But education, being disinterested (not uninterested) in pupils' assent to the content, must be critical of the content in order to be itself.

All of the activities we have been describing may be ethical except indoctrination which is never ethical. This is because the indoctrinator deliberately deprives or seeks to deprive people of part of their humanity, reconstructing their self-hood along lines prescribed solely by the indoctrinator.

But whereas instructing, evangelizing and the others may be ethical, they need not be. You could train somebody to steal, or instruct him in forgery or evangelize him with the religious basis of apartheid. You could train him to perform religious gestures in a manner which paid no attention to his sincerity, or instruct him in a way which made him contemptuous of others, or evangelize him with theological doctrines which would support male supremacy. Such practices would be at odds with the spirit of the content (in this case the Christian faith) but they would not be at odds with the process as such. These processes do not have an ethical control built into them but only become ethically controlled through the influence upon them of their content. Indoctrination has an unethical principle built into it, regardless of its content, and education has an ethical principle built into it, regardless of its content.

Education alone must be ethical by its nature. This is because it supposes a method of treating persons which necessarily holds personhood to be inviolable. It seeks the growth of the person in that which constitutes being human. It places no trust in specific propositions and does not seek to win assent to specific doctrines but it seeks only to seek and to seek again. It is this openness to the truth and to the future through enquiry, and this commitment to the integrity and autonomy of the person which constitute the essentially ethical nature of the relationship between the educator and his pupil. To summarize this point, catechism is normally a perfectly respectable and moral activity. Religious and political groups have a right to offer instruction and nurture in their various tenets to whoever desires them. But the ethical aspects, although not normally absent from these other means of communicating, are integral to the concept of education.

There is a further reason why education must be ethically responsible. This is to do with its attitude towards the authority of its content. The instructor does not have to make decisions about his instruction because the whole of the instruction is guaranteed by authority. This is why instructors get worried if they realize they are not going to 'get through the course'. The ethical responsibility of the instructor is to get through it. But the educator is always involved in making choices about whether the experiences he is introducing are worthwhile, about whether the humanity which inspires his education is true humanity, and how he could tell if it were not. The whole of general education is an ethical problem and specific education, since it is most free and therefore most responsible, is most critically aware of itself as posing ethical problems.

Finally, we may contrast specific education with the other processes we have been considering in so far as its attitude towards authority is different. The other processes recognize the authority of the teaching of the tradition they are conveying. Training recognizes the authority of the mechanical necessity which makes a sequence of operations invariable. In education, however, authority only has a legitimate role when its purpose is to create the conditions which make education possible. These are conditions to do with the authenticity of the persons educating and being educated.[1] The authority of education is thus intrinsic to the person, the authority of the other forms of communication is extrinsic to the person. Extrinsic controls over learning are only compatible with specific education if their intention is to make themselves unnecessary as soon as possible. But if we find forms of extrinsic authority which intend to perpetuate themselves, to keep people in a state of dependence and of childhood for ever, then such authority would be hostile to the spirit of education.

Religious education cannot be other than all that education is, in the sphere of religion. It will be interested in principles, it will be rational, personal, ethical. It will seek to open futures for a pupil but not to determine a particular future for him. It will be critical of the specific content of religion and of the actual claims of religion. It will seek to win the assent of the pupil towards education but not towards religion. It will, however, make assent to religion possible by imparting discrimination and powers of enquiry. But it will not insist upon either assent nor dissent although either may be achieved in a manner appropriate to education.

There is thus a sense in which the religious educator is committed and another sense in which he is neutral. He is committed to the nature of education within the field of religion. This may or may not be combined with commitment to the truth of a given religion. He is neutral about the truth claim of a given religion in the sense that he is disinterested (not uninterested) about its truth claim. He is disinterested about its truth claim in the sense that it is not his object to secure commitment to or rejection of that religion. He is interested in those truth claims in the sense that he wants his pupils to understand them, to realize upon what they are based, to compare them with other claims, and to go on enquiring after them.

We now come to the major problem confronting us in this chapter. In what circumstances may worship and specific education live together?[2]

We have already seen some of the points of tension. We have seen that worship not only entails beliefs but assumes them to be true. Nurture prepares for belief, evangelization summons belief, instruction implants belief, catechism strengthens belief and worship assumes belief. But education scrutinizes belief. It is clear, then, that worship and education cannot take place concurrently.

This, of course, is not the same as saying that worship never teaches or should be expected to teach anything to the worshipper. You may learn a great deal about your faith and yourself whilst worshipping and if you become aware of the fact that you are learning and begin to focus attention on what you may learn then we might say that you were teaching yourself (deliberately maximizing the possibilities of learning). In the same way, a priest might hope that his people would learn a lot from their participation in the sacrament of holy communion and if this intention that they should learn whilst worshipping came to be uppermost in his mind we might then say that he was actively teaching them. But teaching and learning are very general expressions which are used to cover a variety of forms of communication.

When someone is in hospital he may learn a lot and there is a broad sense in which he could say that being in hospital was a truly educational experience. But this is the wide and general sense of 'education'. Even if he participated in discussion with fellow patients and staff which were intentionally educational in the specific sense we have described, it would remain true that these experiences were incidental to his presence in the hospital. The purpose of the hospital is not to teach him, let alone to teach him in the way we have called specific education, but to heal him. Similarly the learning and teaching which take place during worship are either incidental to it and not part of its intention (a man may learn that worship leaves him unmoved!), or they are the product of instruction (a man learns that he is a sinner and that God calls him to repentance as he listens to the New Testament lesson being read) or of nurture (he learns that the worshipping community will support him and befriend him and so he is strengthened in his faith).

But worship and specific education cannot take place at the same time. When we consider education in this specific sense in which we have contrasted it with training and so on, then the priest cannot intend both to lead worship and to specifically educate the same people at the same time. The one act could, however, be intended and interpreted as a worshipful experience by believers present and as an educational experience by non-worshipping learners present for whom it might be a part of a study of religion. Worship can provide matter for education, both when it is observed in order to understand what other people are doing and when one's own worship is reflected upon in retrospect in order to understand what one has done. But it is only when worship becomes matter, content, for education, that the two can coincide. As processes they are fundamentally different.

There is not this tension between worship and training. Whilst worshipping one can be trained to worship, in so far as training is significant and relevant in the worshipping process. One can certainly be instructed whilst worshipping; the attitude of worship and instruction towards their content matter is similar. We recall at this point that instruction requires an agreed content, and that one cannot worship incompatible images of God. The role of this agreement or unanimity, this unequivocal attitude towards its object, links worship and instruction. The words of the hymns instruct and offer worship at the same time without any tension. The same is true of nurture and catechizing. Catechizing may imply a verbal exchange between the catechist and his pupil which will necessitate a pause in the worshipful activities and in that practical sense one cannot worship and be catechized simultaneously, but the difficulty is a practical one and does not reflect any difference in principle between the two which would make them ill at ease with each other. Catechizing may be thought of as a more cognitive activity than worship, or as involving a different set of affections, but there again, the difference between worship and catechizing lies in what they propose to do with the belief, whether to adore or to communicate to another person, rather than indicating a substantially different stance. It is not the business of the catechist to call in question the belief which it is the business of worship to adore, but rather to impress upon the catechumen its adorability.

Although they cannot for reasons of principle take place simultaneously, we have seen that education may follow worship by using worship as its content. Education may also be a preparation for worship but it is important to notice that the intention that worshippers should worship more intelligently, more sincerely or more beautifully is more typical of nurture or catechism than of education. Education, since it does not intend to deepen commitment to the content of the propositions with which it deals but only to the methods by which it deals with its content, cannot intend to make worship more sincere. This would mean that education was seeking to deepen commitment to the beliefs upon which worship is founded and which provide the content of worship. Education, however, seeks not to deepen commitment to these beliefs but to subject them to scrutiny.

It is possible that education might intend to make worship more intelligent, but that will be understood by education in terms of education, not in the terms which worship might require. To worship intelligently, as worship understands it, is to worship the Lord God and not Baal and to worship in spirit and in truth. But to worship intelligently, as education understands it, is to pass through a period of reflection in which you are exposed to the possibility that there might be neither God nor Baal to worship, or if they be, then they might not be worthy of worship.

Education necessarily puts the possibility of worshipping at risk, since it scrutinizes the cognitive associations of worship and the propriety of the emotional reactions to those cognitions which worship expresses. But the reverse is not necessarily the case. Christian worship does not necessarily put the possibility of educating at risk, since it does not scrutinize the presuppositions of education as long as education is understood in the way described here. There might be other understandings of education which theology (but not worship immediately) might scrutinize in a critical spirit, but the worship we describe, and the education as well, spring from deeper common sources. Worship is committed to the same ideals which, in its own way, education is intended to foster. Far from putting it at risk, Christian worship then ought to enhance the possibility of educating.

If someone tried to make his whole life literally worship, so that all periods of reflection upon the nature of worship and its object were absorbed completely by the demands of unqualified adoration, then such a life would be one of fanatical idolatry. Worship would have over-reached itself. It would have destroyed education along with itself, for in consuming a whole life in this way worship would no longer constitute an appropriate response to God. For God is logos.

There is then a remaining tension between worship and education in spite of the fact that the same person may at different times be both a worshipper and a subject of education. This tension may be summarized by saying that worship is committed to its content and is passionate and adoring while education is detached from its content and is enquiring and reflective.

Yet there are links between worship and specific education which have been suggested but not explored. The concept of specific education which has been discussed is not self contained and autonomous. It is not simply true by definition, as if education must always be as we have described it and logically could not be otherwise. The total process of general education is complex and we have seen that it is a cluster or family of types of communication. Not everything which goes on in schools is or ought to be education in the specific sense with which we have contrasted it with training and socializing.

There may well be parts of the world or times in the past when this family of processes called general education was arranged with a different order of emphases or where one or more element was lacking, even the element which is here selected as the heart and defining centre of the whole series. Even if this sense of specific education as being critical, rational, personal, ethical, person centred, and so on, were lacking, we could still correctly describe the child rearing, the training, the cultural initiation and so on of preliterate, tribal peoples as their general educational procedures. Our understanding of the educational processes is thus relative and is conditioned by a wide variety of cultural, historical and political factors. No attempt is being made to claim universal validity for them.

Among the many influences which mould the concepts of education are views of the nature and destiny of man. There are as many views of general education in the West as there are views of man. This is seen in the Jesuit education of the sixteenth and seventeenth centuries, the education advocated by Rousseau in the eighteenth century, that offered by the English public school in the nineteenth century and that associated with Dewey in the twentieth century, all of which are rather clear examples of an ideal of man creating and sustaining an ideal of education.[3] Of contemporary educationalists, Paulo Freire is outstanding as one whose educational programmes are from the start to finish worked out consistently from a view of the nature of man.[4]

The essential feature of human being from the point of view of education is that it is unfinished. The unfinished nature of being human indicates that unlike those creatures in the animal and plant world whose development passes through more or less fixed stages until it arrives at a point of maturity where the nature of the entity can be seen as complete, fully formed, and perfectly expressed, man's present moment of being is won out of the choices, selected and unselected influences, meetings, crises which have marked each previous moment and which in turn will suffer further selection as the future is imagined and prepared for.[5] There are certain respects in which human being reaches a point where it is finished. Physical development is finished at a certain age. An individual receives from the past of his society certain skills and attitudes which when he has secured them for himself constitute a kind of finished status. This is particularly evident in processes of training, where the training can be truly finished when the pupil has mastered the skill. He cannot be trained to a greater degree of perfection (which is not to say that he will not go on improving) and is thus finished. But most of the respects in which human life can be described as finished refer to stages of life. You finish your schooling, or your career, or your adolescence.

But being human itself is never finished because humanity is achieved as well as conferred. The form of being human (the body) is conferred. Physical growth is irresistible. But the essence of being human always has a further horizon. Because the being of being human is concealed in the future and because our orientation towards that future is directed (but not entirely determined) by the past, we can summarize the peculiarity of human being by saying that it is historical. It is the meeting of the times (past, present and future) in the human consciousness, held together by the imagination which indicates the historical nature of humanity.[6]

It is towards the unfinished nature of man that education points and this is why we can say that education, unlike training, instructing and indoctrinating, is never finished. There are criteria for determining when the indoctrination of an individual is finished. Does the indoctrinated person continue to hold the belief or belief system regardless of the evidence? Does he display emotional hostility towards any counter suggestion? Similarly, there are ways of telling if instructing is finished. Instruction always deals with a specific content and when that content has been covered and the student has demonstrated his ability to reproduce it and to understand it then the purpose of the instruction is complete and that part of the person which is created by the instruction is finished.

But to what part of the person is specific education directed? We have seen that it has no purpose other than to make further learning possible, that it enquires and goes on enquiring and that in doing so it is guided by certain beliefs about the person. Education, then, is never finished, not in the sense in which people say 'You learn something new every day' which can mean simply that there is always something new about which to receive instruction, but in the sense that personhood is never finished. If instruction cannot be finished, it is because man is mortal — there is not enough time. But education cannot be finished because man is immortal. There are no limits to the spirit. We are talking here about the ontology of the human, and about education as reflecting that ontology. We have no criteria for the finishing of education because we have no criteria for the finishing of man. But when we select imaginatively what we will become in the future we are selecting guide lines for the process of education. We have then criteria for the process of education, but as long as there is a future horizon for man, education will never be complete. In old age, the future is fore-shortened, but although the process of winning one's humanity can be ossified at any age, there is no age or stage of life which cannot have its future extended. Perhaps only in the moment when martyrdom is chosen and the future thus foreclosed can education be said to be finished.

Man as finished and unfinished is only one of the many strands from which the concept of specific education outlined in this chapter is drawn. Currents of European thought as diverse as renaissance humanism, eighteen-century rationalism and modern existentialism contribute to it. If the result can be summarized in the broadest terms we may say that here man is viewed as becoming personal, rational and ethical; he is to become free and responsible, constituting his own nature by his capacity to transcend his past and his environment; he is thus world-creating, imagining, and he grows in relationships of love.

Education is thus man-centred ontologically and child-centered only methodologically. The structure and nature of education points towards human formation (here we see the link between education and nurture which we noticed

before) and it is interested in childhood in so far as this is a
critical period of formation and requires a particular method.
Flowing from such a view of man, the function of education
(stated in another way) is to facilitate the formation of such
men.

We are now in a position to distinguish between specific
education and pedagogy. Pedagogy is applied education and
education is applied philosophical anthropology. To put it
more exactly, pedagogy is educational method applied to
children; the ideals and norms which guide this method are
derived from reflections about the status of being human.[7]

There are times and places when education loses its
anthropological self-awareness. Forgetting the image of man
which inspires it, it no longer contributes to man as
unfinished but concentrates upon the limited finishing of
pupils. Then education becomes vocational training or social
class reinforcement ('finishing schools'), or more bluntly,
education becomes schooling. But even here, views of man
are held out and the schools are subscribing to them. Indeed,
perhaps the most rapid way for the schools to succumb to
views of man which are racialist, totalitarian, or which aim to
manufacture men for the manufacturing society is to
persuade the schools to accept narrow understandings of
their function and to teach the teachers to concentrate upon
strictly 'educational matters' such as methods of teaching
children to read.[8] Education as a whole is then thought of
by the teacher as a conglomerate of such techniques and then
teaching becomes a trade and education becomes practically
autonomous as a discipline. By obscuring its humane depth in
this or other ways education can easily be made to serve the
interests of alien and dehumanizing views of man and so in
claiming its autonomy education loses its freedom. But in
insisting on its dependence upon philosophical anthropology
it retains this awareness and thus its capacity to reflect and
regenerate the image of man of which it understands itself as
inevitably the counter image.

Amongst the main sources of the view of man which we
are considering is the Judeao-Christian-Islamic view of man as
being in the image of God. Man is described in the opening
chapters of the Bible as the lord of creation who in naming
the creatures confers identity, order and rationality upon the

world. The world is capable of bearing that impression because it too comes from the hand and bears the image of God. Man's free, rational and creative life in community is founded in, guaranteed by, and understood through the nature of God who has expressed himself and graciously given himself in creating man and the world.

There are, of course, many theologies of education resting upon various interpretations of man. Common to many of them is the question whether the view of man involved in a Christian theology of education must be Pelagian. Does education represent itself as a human technique for the perfectability of man? If so, what room is left for the operation of divine grace and does education become the same as salvation?

The appearance of Pelagianism, the hint that man can live without sin if he will, arises from the fact that education has been related particularly to man as unfinished. It is man as he might become rather than man as he is which has been emphasized. This has led to a stress on man as becoming more rational and more loving. These, we saw, were guidelines for the expansion of human being. Man as unfinished is hopeful man, with a future in which he will be more human. Had man been described with greater emphasis upon his finished status, then we would have had a gloomier impression, for the finished in man represents at least in part the rigid structures inherited from the individual and the collective past, the deposits of habit, the limitations of outlook, the areas of a person's life which, having determined that they are now finished, are not susceptible any longer to criticism, to growth, to change. The same point has been made by reference to the idea of the image of God. The image of God is the dreamed past just as finished man is the fractured present, and unfinished man is the hoped for future. 'Image of God' and 'unfinished' both point away from the experienced ambiguity and fragmentation of man's present claimed self-sufficiency towards an ideal of what man might become. They represent more than an ideal; they indicate that which man most faithfully is called to be; they are ontological categories.

The concept of the image is taken from the first chapter of Genesis. In the third chapter we read of the disruption of the image, of the fall, and its curse. If we took our bearings entirely from the story of the fall and insisted that man can no longer remember the image from which he declined nor long for its reformation, if, in other words, the fall means that man is ineluctably bound into the straits of his actual existence and has no norms by which to realize that this present actuality does not represent all that his being human means, so that he were unable to imagine receiving his humanity again from God, then there could be no question of self-salvation nor presumably of divine salvation either, and no question of education in the sense we understand it.

Our conception of education is thus not unaware of the fall and of sin but it refuses to admit that the fallen imagination is so fallen that it can no longer dream of what was, nor imagine what might become. As far as the means of education are concerned, the ideals of human being which inspire education are for Christian theology informed by faith in God. Since man in the image of God lies behind our view of education, God himself as a gracious creator and loving redeemer is the source of Christian thinking about education. For the Christian, revelation is integral to education. Revelation is itself the gift of God. Only when we turn to the strictly technical aspects of pedagogy do we come to skills which lie entirely within the unaided human capacity. But since these skills must be informed by the deeper view of man which is given to Christian faith in revelation, if they are to contribute to education, and not merely be a pedagogy of training, then even the selection and operation and criticism of the pedagogical skills themselves cannot be conducted by the Christian educator without reference to the self-giving grace of God. These are the general lines along which a charge of Pelagianism levelled against this view of education might be rebutted.

In our discussion so far of the relations between worship and education we have located three levels. First we have the level of education itself, then that of the view of man which it expresses; and finally the idea of God in whose gift is the being of man. Worship is related immediately to the adoration of the deepest level, the divine.

In distinguishing these three levels, there is a sense in which we are only discussing the history of ideas. We are, up to a point, merely observing that historically certain ideas about man from the ancient Middle East have, through Judaism, Islam and above all Christianity, flowed into the formation of western concepts of education.

But we are talking theology as well as history of ideas. We are affirming the present power of the concept of God to support and clarify the views of both man and education. This, however, does not mean that we could or should attempt to construct a chain of argument from the deepest to the upper level in such a way that those who accept the conception of education outlined here must also accept belief in God. Our intention is not to offer any reason to the atheist educator for believing in God but simply to show to the Christian educator that the relationship between education and faith in God, and in turn between worshipping God and educating, may be one of harmony not conflict, provided the distinct nature of the various processes is kept clearly in mind.

The atheist educator may accept the view of education outlined here and argue that the ideals of love and freedom which it entails are values greater than which there are none by which they can be justified and that the ideal of man which this education supposes is in that sense chosen in faith. Or the atheist educator may find some other way of defending the view of man involved in the educational quest. This second level of man must be insisted upon in order to safeguard education itself. But it is enough for the Christian educator to show that although not logically required by levels one and two the idea of God at level three is not incompatible with education, that indeed it supports it, and in this way to integrate his religious faith with his professional practice and ideals.

Now, in Christian faith, man is man most truly when he is responding appropriately to the God in whose image he is and is to become. And it is the task of education to build up and restore man. Worship and education are thus both forms of appropriate response to God. Worship, however, responds by adoring God consciously, immediately and directly. It has no intention other than this explicit adoration. Specific education, thought of now as a form of appropriate response to God, is an example of the third sense of 'secular worship' discussed above. It is the 'worship' (a metaphorical sense of the word) of the offering of one's daily life and work to God. During this offering one may not be thinking of God at all; indeed, it would be impossible to think of God very much whilst teaching a class of lively children, and because it is impossible literally to worship God without thinking constantly of him, this kind of worship must be a metaphorical extension of the concept of worship. This is what is meant by saying that the worship offered by the Christian teacher in his teaching is not conscious; it is not conscious of thinking about God. In another sense, it is conscious 'worship', in that the teaching is in general sustained by faith in God and intends to glorify God by the quality of the work done rather than by deliberately addressing God. We may put the distinction like this: all worship in the Christian tradition is worship of God but not all education (even of the kind we describe as specific education) is secular worship of God, for only believers in God literally worship him, while believers and non-believers of all sorts are educators and share in various ways and with various rationales in proposing the view of man which education requires. The daily work of a teacher can only be described as his worship of God if it expresses an orientation towards that which is literally worshipped at some time or other.

It is essential to the Christian educator that this harmonious relationship between education and worship should be maintained. This must be done in such a way as not to deny the distinctions between them, and to recognize that at times this may become a real tension. But the most usual danger today is not that the tension between education and worship becomes unbearable but that education and worship tend to be absorbed into one another. The Christian teacher who tries to make the secular worship of his daily work into explicit and literal worship, by, for example, offering prayer audibly with his class before and after lessons, or by encouraging his pupils to worship during his classes, will probably find that education will tend to turn into nurture or even evangelism and if this is pursued into his life as a whole, his life may tend to become idolatrous, since it will lack the critical detachment afforded by education. The element of logos which is part of the appropriate response to the

Christian God would have been lost, and so the response would no longer be to the God of Christian faith but to a totalitarian deity whose absolute prerogatives as creator have swamped all autonomy and rational development in the creature. Such a Christian would have become a slave, not a son.

On the other hand, should his education swallow up his worship so that there is no longer any explicit acknowledgement of God nor any immediate submission to him, he is in danger of losing the very values which undergird his work as a Christian educator. He would have ceased to give direct expression to the supreme worthship of God and thus his Christian faith as a teacher in man as the image of God would be impaired. The task of the Christian in education is to glorify God by the excellence of his educational work. Paul said that whether a Christian eats or drinks, he does it for the glory of God, and he almost added that nevertheless when a Christian eats, he eats, when he drinks, he drinks. One does not glorify God instead of eating, and non-Christians also eat. So it is with education.

We have remarked that specific education by its nature may place worship at risk. This need not alarm the Christian educator. A religion centred around a faith-response to a gracious revelation is always at risk. The element of risk in Christian worship is built into its context in faith, since faith is not sight and always involves the possibility of being mistaken. Christian theology, like Christian education, must at times put faith at extra risk in the effort to be obedient to faith itself and in order to retain intellectual integrity.

But whereas theology is the servant of faith and challenges faith in the name of deeper faith, education although informed and supported by faith is not the servant of faith. If it were the servant of faith, it would cease to be education and would become nurture and catechism. Education follows its own norms even though since they flow from its view of man it is not the originator of them. It must be true to its norms of critical, ethical, person-centred rationality. Such education, although the offspring of Christian faith, is no longer a child of faith but a fully grown son threatening (as some may see it) to destroy its parent. As theology destroys naive faith, so specific education destroys cautious and encapsulated nurture.

It is at this point that many Christians ask whether faith, already under strain from so many sources, can afford the additional risk to potentially Christian children and young people which education presents. The British religious education scene offers a particularly interesting example of this at the present time, for whereas during the 1960s the initiative was in the hands of Christian religious educators and the influences upon state religious education were from Christian church sources, we now see that the tide has turned and is running the other way. Christian schools and the education offered within the churches are now exposed to pressures about the nature of the educational process coming from the development of a vigorous secularized religious education within the state system. Ought we not, many church men might wonder, content ourselves with nurture which has as one of its direct aims the strengthening of worship?

There is no doubt that this would be a perfectly legitimate procedure in churches and in some church schools. But would it be the most advisable one? In the Middle Ages, when there was almost no education in the specific sense described here, nurture was effective in establishing life-long habits of worship and faith because a church member might go all his life without meeting an intelligent adult who would disagree radically with his religious views. In a pluralist society this is no longer the case. This is why enclosed nurture has become ineffective. Nurture guards, protects, guides in the traditionally accepted way. If alternative positions are presented, they are looked at by apologetics, to see how they might be answered; the nurturer himself stands in the faith into which the young are nurtured and his own model is the same as one which is set before them. But all over the Christian world authoritative content-centred catechesis and faith-centred protective nurture are giving way to more critical approaches under the pressure of pluralism.

In a plural situation, where believers are living in daily contact with people of other political and religious commitments, or of none, there are only two possible ways for general Christian upbringing. The first possibility is to rear the young and prepare the prospective church members in isolation from the rest of the community by establishing

either physical or ideological barriers. The acute distress
caused by the cognitive clash experienced by a minority faith
in a non-supportive environment can be alleviated by creating
such a community. Only in such circumstances can nurture
be effective, but the price is not worth it. Adults nurtured
in this way can never become incarnated into the society of
their times. The church which takes this step can never
become the body of Christ in the world.

The other option is education, in the specific sense in
which we contrast it with nurture. We need to ask not
whether we can afford to educate but whether we can afford
not to accept the risks of education. For the future of
Christian faith depends upon the formation of adults who
have knowingly chosen it in the presence of understood
alternatives.[9] Education by its nature cannot guarantee or
even intend the formation of such adults, but nothing else
has any chance at all of forming them.

So the wheel has come at last full circle. Education is the
product (along with other influences) of Christian faith. Now
Christian faith increasingly depends upon education (amongst
other influences) for its own reproduction even although
education cannot intend to reproduce Christian faith. If
Christianity is to remain an option for people in an
increasingly open ideological world, education is likely to
become increasingly the most significant experience after
which that option may be usefully, realistically and genuinely
accepted.

Earlier in this chapter we described religious specific
education as being all that specific education is, in the sphere
of religion. Since that point of our discussion, we have
considered the relation between Christian faith and education
rather more fully. So we come now to the question: What is
Christian education?

Christian education cannot refer to an education the
purpose of which is to create Christians, or to confirm people
in their Christianity. This would be properly described as
Christian nurture. Education has no aim other than further
learning.[10]

Christian education could refer to that part of the
educational curriculum which deals with Christianity. In this
sense we might speak of history or geography education. But

this meaning is better conveyed by the expression Christian Studies.

Finally, Christian education could refer to a Christian quality permeating education. This is usually taken to mean a quality such as to create or nurture Christians but we can now see that that is not a possible meaning of specific education. Christian education is therefore nothing but education (whether its curriculum content be religion or not, Christianity or not) in the specific sense we have discussed. It is Christian in so far as it is sustained, supported and flows from Christian faith. It is Christian in so far as Christians intend it to be so.

Is the difference between education and Christian education merely a matter of the intention of the educator? If he is a Christian, then his education, inspired by Christian faith, is Christian education, not only without ceasing to be education, but (because of the way Christian faith supports education) being more truly and fully education. Certainly, the intention of the educator is of vital importance. In this respect, the parallel with eating holds good. Pagan eating and Christian eating may not be observably different. Eating to the glory of God is an intention. Eating is still eating, however, even when Christians do it.

But the analogy is not wholly satisfactory. Education is not always the same everywhere and no matter who does it. The general education of the eskimoes and the Welsh and the Navajo Indians is all different. There are forms of general education which lack entirely the concept of specific education as developed here. The education offered by those who hold one of the various Christian views of man will therefore be different not only in its intention but in its substance. This could be illustrated in detail by asking what concepts of education would flow from Islamic faith or from Plato or from Stoic or Epicurian philosophy.

The way in which specific education flows from Christian faith may be illustrated if we consider that the general education (and not simply specific education) offered by the Christian communities is rightly dedicated to the finishing of man. Christian instruction, for example, can never be finished (and this distinguishes it from other instructions) because Christian instruction is never about a finished past (Heb.

11.40). The openness which characterizes even instruction (when it is Christian) springs from the unpredictability of history, and when we say that Christianity is a historical religion we do not simply mean that it rests upon events which once took place in history but that it is historical in the way that human being is historical: it is a point of existence at which the past, the present and the future are brought together in the consciousness of time: this constitutes the historical nature of Christian faith. Consider Christian instruction about Christmas. This, as distinct from New Year which celebrates the passage of time, is the celebration of the breaking into time of the eternal. This can only be celebrated if each Christmas, and every day, Christians are aware of standing in the presence of the eternal now. To instruct young people about Christmas in such a way as to lock it in the past, to present it as a finished event, is to reduce it to the celebration of time alone, and the past alone at that. To be adapted to the nature of Christian faith in Christmas, instruction must therefore be open to the creation of a fresh future. Christian revelation can only be received if it is renewed in the reception.[11] The instructor in Christian theology is, in the most real sense, actually making new theology in the process of instruction. There can thus be no predictable Christian instruction, for the instruction renews itself in unforeseen ways.

The same is true of Christian training. There can be no invariable sequence of religious operations, whether these be intellectual, devotional or liturgical. This could only be asserted if the status of the Holy Spirit as the Lord and Giver of life was denied.

It is qualities such as these which are concentrated in the notion of specific education. Christians need claim no monopoly of the concept or of the practice. He that is not against us is on our side, and no educator, Christian or not, should speak ill of these ideals. It is the task of the Christian in education not to seek to corner the market, or to be concerned if the pagans also exorcize the demons, but to exercise a prophetic creativity between Christian faith and education, so that the concept and practice of education is always being refreshed and renewed from the resources which the Christian faith holds.

4 *Worship and the Secularization of Religious Education*

The assumptions behind religious education in publicly maintained schools in the British Isles have changed more in the last ten years than in the previous one hundred years. We have seen how the moralistic, liturgical formality of the nineteenth century gave way to the religious nurture movement in the 1920s. In the nineteenth century there was no distinction (even on the timetable in many cases) between worship and classroom instruction; in the religious nurture movement of the twentieth century, worship and instruction became twin agents for the fostering of religious faith and practice and worship occupied a secure place at the summit of a prevailing philosophy of religion in the school. During assembly the school expressed its truest nature as an alleged Christian community.

Religious education in the state schools has now been removed from its traditional context within religious faith and devotion. The results for school worship are nothing short of disastrous. This will appear as we examine the changes which have taken place. The changes can be summarized simply by remarking that religious education has been secularized.

A characteristic of the nurturing period of religious education was that the subject was sponsored by the religious bodies. This is illustrated by the fact that until 1944 religious instruction in county schools was not subject to inspection by the state inspectorate but by officials appointed by the local authority, many of whom were clergy. The origins of the British system of school inspection are to be found in the medieval visitations of both churches and schools carried out by ecclesiastical officials.[1] The voluntary educational societies of the eighteenth and early nineteenth centuries were rigidly inspected by the various denominations. All teachers in Anglican charity schools had to be approved by the Anglican clergy.[2] With the giving of government financial aid to voluntary schools from 1833, government inspectors were empowered to include religious teaching in their inspections, and could withhold the government grant if it were not satisfactory, but it became 'increasingly clear that government inspectors were becoming, more and more, secular officers . . .',[3] and the religious authorities continued and indeed increased their systems of inspection of their own denominational schools in spite of the creation of the government inspectorate.

From 1870, when the state system of schools was founded, until the end of the century, Board School inspectors (but not the inspectors of the central government) were entitled to inspect the religious teaching given in accordance with the syllabus laid down by the local Board of Education. Sometimes a 'clerical gentleman was employed by the Board to do this on behalf of the Board',[4] and in this way the traditional inspection of religious teaching by ecclesiastical authorities managed to survive even the birth of the state school system. The larger Boards, however, tended to appoint an inspector qualified to inspect religion. The HMIs might ask to see the reports made out by these local Board inspectors.[5]

This situation was continued into the twentieth century. Under the 1921 Education Act HMIs were strictly forbidden to enquire into the religious teaching of any school[6] and with the growing power of the teaching profession, the custom of inspection by clergymen became a matter of some controversy. The 1929 Report of the Church Assembly comments rather coyly: 'The LEAs have the right, through their inspectors, to make enquiries as to the standard of religious knowledge in their schools, and we think it desirable *that this right should be more widely used*'[7] (My italics). In some cases, representatives of both the Church of England and of the Free Churches were commissioned by the LEAs to undertake this work. '. . . in some areas arrangements are in force under which both provided and non-provided schools are periodically inspected in religious subjects by a joint body of clergymen or other persons representing the different denominations'.[8] The National Union of Teachers began to

protest against this practice. 'The NUT is strongly opposed to
the appointment of members of the clerical profession to
supervise and inspect the work of teachers. We do not admit
their competence for the task.'[9] 'The policy of appointing
local ministers to inspect the religious teaching . . . does not
commend itself to the members of the teaching profession.'[10]

In order to remove this offence and to bring the teaching
of religion into parity with other subjects, the Spens report
recommended in 1938 that religious teaching should be open
to inspection by the government inspectorate.[11] This was
supported by the churches and became law in 1944. Through
the fifth schedule of the 1944 Act, however, the churches
continued to create and thus to control although not actually
to inspect the teaching of religion in state schools. So, in
England and Wales (the areas of the British Isles affected by
the 1944 Act) the churches were able to bring about an
exchange in which they gave up their rights regarding
inspection to the HMIs in exchange for statutory power over
the Agreed Syllabuses, thus ensuring greater control (one is
reminded of the role of the syllabuses before 1920 *vis à vis*
inspection of schools) and greater prestige for what there was
to control.[12] 'Inspection by the clergy still takes place in
Northern Ireland, an area where critical and descriptive
religious teaching has made but slow progress against nurture
controlled by the churches.'

We have seen how the rise of the Agreed Syllabus
represented a new stage in nurture because it granted a closer
relationship with the sponsoring bodies.[13] So clergy now
co-operated with teachers in the production of syllabuses and
it is interesting to remember the very great influence
exercised at this point by some of the great clerical
headmasters of the forties, such as Spencer Leeson.[14] The
agreement between the churches made it possible for
instruction to emerge. In the nineteenth century it was
disagreement on doctrine, even on the part of Anglicans in
Anglican schools, which prevented anything more than such
elementary items as the Book of Common Prayer and the
Apostles' Creed being taught. Instruction can only be
effective when the content which it is the business of
instruction to pass on is authoritative, and it can only
become authoritative when it is agreed upon by the instruct-

ing parties. So in the 1920s and 1930s mere textual exegesis with historical and geographical comments and moralizing applications gave way to Christian doctrine and the syllabuses became more theological. The Bible as a book about faith intended to produce and maintain faith dominated the subject with new vigour in the forty years which followed.

It was after the 1944 Act that sponsorship reached its climax.[15] The religious bodies comprised two of the four committees which drew up an Agreed Syllabus and each committee possessed the power of veto. Religious education thus represents one of the final pockets of ecclesiastical domination over a sphere of secular expertise, namely, education. By the secularization of religious education is therefore meant in the first place its freeing from ecclesiastical control and the serving of ecclesiastical interests, the latter including the fostering of the faith represented by the ecclesiastical sponsors.[16]

The Act merely ratified an existing consensus and the secularization which we have seen in religious education in very recent years has not been the product of legislation either. The forces at work in the subject have operated independently of the Act and have had the effect of reducing the religious sections of the Act to a mere formality. Embarrassed by the power at their disposal, the producers of Agreed Syllabuses have insisted that they contain no more than suggestions, that they are merely advice offered to teachers,[17] but it has become impossible to avoid the problem that the creation of a syllabus by persons other than the teachers themselves is no longer acceptable to the teaching profession. Many teachers, especially secondary specialists, would consider it an admission of their own incompetence if they were unable to produce their own syllabus for their own distinctive situations. Through teachers' centres, working parties and projects of various kinds, material has been produced within many areas which has been more influential than the official syllabus.[18] Accepted procedures of curriculum development have now overtaken the law regarding the production of Agreed Syllabuses, leaving the law a hollow shell.[19]

The religious education renaissance of the early and middle sixties can now be seen as the final attempt to revive the nurture model. The aim was to find more effective ways of

making Christian faith meaningful and relevant for the
young. Even as late as 1965 there was no distinction to make
between Christian and religious education.[20]

But the seeds of secularization were there in the 'religious
education revolution' of those years. The growing realization
that the nurturing intention in religious education was failing
was itself a heavy blow to the Christian religious educator.
The movement away from doctrinal instruction towards open
discussion and life-centred methods was reinforced by the
realization that much of the biblical and theological teaching
in the syllabuses was unsuitable for young children.

Not, however, until the emergence in strength of the
movement for the study of world religions in school in the
last three or four years has the full impact of secularization
hit religious education. At first, in the thirties, the non-
Christian faiths were taught mainly in the context of
Christian missions.[21] Only slowly and cautiously did the
study of the actual beliefs of the other religions appear, and
then nearly always in sixth-form apologetics. The formation
in 1969 of the Shap Working Party for World Religions in
Schools must be considered an event of first rank importance
in British religious education, since for the first time religions
other than Christianity were taken seriously as part of
religious education. It is a striking paradox that this
affirmation of a distinctive religious content for the subject
should have the effect of bringing the secularization process
to a head. How has this taken place?

First, it is now clearly seen that the religions have ceased
to be the sponsors of religious education and have become
instead the objects of religious study. The religions are now
the phenomena which are the concern of this part of the
curriculum. But which religions shall be studied and how is
increasingly the preserve of the teacher.

No religion or religious group has found this change in
status easy to understand or to accept. When for more than a
thousand years you have had the power to bind and loose in
education, it is not nice to be told you are now an interesting
object of study. Churches with their own school systems
(notably the Roman Catholics and the Anglicans) have
perhaps been slowest and most reluctant to react, partly of
course because it remains possible to continue a sponsoring
relationship towards the religious education offered in

schools which are themselves sponsored. But so strong are the influences coming from the vastly larger state sector that the nurture model seems likely to shrink even in the voluntary schools.

Nevertheless, it has been mainly Christian educators who have advocated the secularization of religion in schools, even although ably supported by humanist criticism. To the adherents of the great Asian faiths the idea of a critical religious education not designed to foster faith sometimes appears alien, both to traditions of religion and education. On the other hand, there is a sense in which being relatively recent arrivals in Britain (with the exception of Judaism) and not expecting to receive any attention at the hands of state religious education, the non-Christian faiths have found it easier to accept that their beliefs and customs may be of interest to young people who do not necessarily intend to adopt them, while Christian clergy, as the inheritors of the privileges of nurture within the state system, have sometimes found the changed attitudes of religious educators and pupils a source of hurt and confusion.

The second way in which the arrival of the world religions has heightened the secularization crisis of religious education is an extension and a consequence of this. In 1969 and 1970 it became increasingly common for religious educators to distinguish between Christian education and religious education. The latter was reserved for the subject of the curriculum dealing with religion. The former was used to describe Christian nurture, or to describe education as a whole when considered in the light of the Christian faith and its implications,[22] or (less commonly) to describe that part of the subject of the curriculum which dealt with the Christian religion specifically. But these distinctions were being made at a time when Christianity was still the only religion studied in detail, and the contrast between Christian education and religious education was not intended to refer to Christianity and other religions but to nurturing aims (or confessional aims as they are sometimes called) and the aims of a critical, descriptive religious education which would be justified on educational grounds.

In the light of the appearance on the syllabus of the other world faiths, it is now necessary to go a good deal further than the distinction between Christian and religious education. It must now be seen that there is no more necessary or more intimate relationship *in principle* between Christianity and religious education in the state schools than there is between Islam and religious education. The problem of what the Christian faith has to say about religious education is now no different *in kind* from the question of what it might have to say about history education or science education, although because of the partial overlap of subject matter, the relationship is rather more complex in the case of religious education. Islam, similarly, must explore its own implications for education and for the subjects of the curriculum. Behind this insistence lies a question of justice. For if the state is to offer religious education, it must offer it to all regardless of creed and colour. The demand that non-Christians and members of other religions shall take advantage of the notorious escape clauses in the 1944 Act (themselves the most eloquent testimony to the intention of the state to provide for the compulsory nurture of children in Christianity)[23] can no longer be sustained in an increasingly pluralistic state.[24] The question whether under the Act the Local Education Authorities have the responsibility to provide for the education of Islamic and Hindu young people as well as for Christians and those of no religious tradition must be answered in the affirmative. This decision must be made if religion is to remain on the curriculum at all, and it clearly carries with it the implication that Christianity and the other religions shall have a similar relationship towards this subject.

But is this possible? We have seen that specific education is not only fully compatible with and supported by Christian faith, but is in part at least a product of Christian faith. Unless the same can be said of, for example, Islam, then there would be a relationship between education and Christianity which would not be true of education and Islam.

Let us suppose that enquiry were to show that Islam *is* also fully compatible and supportive of specific education and that the ideals of specific education flow at least partly from the Islamic tradition. Then the relationship between Christianity and Islam towards education (and thus religious education) would be similar in principle but different in detail in so far as Christianity and Islam are similar in some respects and different in others. The notion of man as being made in the image of God, common to both faiths, might be a point at which the educational consequences would be similar (although even on the doctrine of the image of God, there are differences between Christianity and Islam), but if there were educational conclusions to be drawn from doctrines distinctive of Christianity (such as the trinity) then this might suggest a different relationship. These differences would be matters for co-operation and continued dialogue and not for fundamental clash regarding education just so long as both faiths agreed in sustaining a religious education which would have the features described in our second and third chapters.

Let us suppose that the reason Christianity supports specific education is in fact because of doctrines peculiar to Christianity, such as the resurrection (the living Lord leading from the future and calling man to his future), the Holy Spirit (revelation is not finished but the Spirit leads into further truth) and the idea of historical and personal revelation as being the secret of openness, thus indicating that Christian doctrine is never a complete and finished structure. Let us suppose that the Islamic idea of tradition is such that revelation is fixed and final in sacred writings and that instruction is the only mode of communication proper to those writings. Then the relationship between Christianity and education would be different from that between Islam and education. Christian religious educators would then be inviting Muslims to share in an educational project which flowed from Christian faith but was not compatible with Islamic faith.[25]

Muslim theologians and educators who are interested in this problem might enquire as to whether the tension between Islam and education (supposing there were such tension) was intrinsic to Islam and ineluctable or whether it was simply a feature of a particular stage or type of Islam which could be overcome by theological reflection and social development. The Christianity of 1870 was more at home with instruction than with specific education, but this tension is being resolved by theological and social changes within Christianity. Perhaps the same might be true of Islam. Perhaps Islam can take criticism as well as (or better than) Christianity, but it may lack an inbuilt principle of criticism. Perhaps it has not produced a critical model of education. In that case, Islam could accept criticism but not produce it.

Then there would at least be no question of education proving more destructive for Islam than for Christianity and up to that point, education would have no favourites.

But *even if* it were the case that the relationship between Christianity and education were friendly and that between Islam and education were hostile, so that there was not the same relationship in fact or in principle between Christianity and education and between Islam and education, it would still be the case that within religious education Christianity would be treated in no more favourable a manner than Islam, that religious education would be just as criticial of Christianity as it would be of Islam, that Islam would be appreciated as deeply as Christianity would be. For just as education cannot in principle exclude from its survey an ideology like fascism, which would destroy education if it gained the upper hand, so education gives no special place to Christianity even though Christianity supports education and fascism destroys it. In this way, education, like justice, is blindfolded and has a sharp sword. Education, like prophecy, is no less harsh towards Israel than towards the nations, even although it is Israel and not the nations which produces the prophets.

But what if it were the case, that although education in principle has no favourites, the results of education were, in fact, better for Christianity than for Islam (to continue the earlier example)? We have said that although education cannot seek to make Christians it may be that Christians will emerge from education. Is this also true of Islam and the other faiths? Now, it may well be the case that there are certain closed and fanatical forms of religion (both within Christianity and beyond it) which can never be entered through education, and there may be other forms of religion, more loving, more enquiring (both within Christianity and beyond it) which are entered most usefully through education. This, however, is not the concern of education. Education cannot be deterred by the thought that it might be unsettling to believers in a flat earth, or to believers in astrology, or to any naive and simplistic view of the world. The intentions of education must be neutral as between various schools of thought and ideologies (guided, however, by its view of man). The intention of education cannot be to promote Christian faith; this must be adhered to regardless of the consequences. So in principle, there can be no closer relationship between the matter or content of education and Christianity than between any other faith — there can be no Christian sponsorship, no seeking for the creation of faith in doctrines distinctive or peculiar to Christianity (the view of man upon which education rests is not the peculiar property of Christianity, but faith in Christ as Lord is peculiar to Christianity). What the result of this intention will actually be for the welfare and prosperity of the various faiths is not education's concern, for education has no aim other than further learning.

What is the implication, however, of the thought that education is guided by its view of man? Does that not mean that education must be closer to humanism, to liberal Christianity, and farther from fascism and capitalism? Let us distinguish between the formal principles of education, the material principles and finally the methods of education. In its formal principles, the actual concept of specific education as set out in chapter 3, there are closer links between Christianity and education than between fascism and educa-tion. Education is in its formal principles not neutral but is guided by a view of man, a view which is denied by fascism, and maintained by Christianity. The material principles of education are to do with the selection of content for curricula. Here education is neutral. It has no favourites. Even the view of man which it expresses is exposed to criticism and comparison with other views of man. It is because the formal principles of education are *not* neutral that the material principles *are* neutral.[26] The open enquiry, and questioning of everything, which leads to an equal treatment of the various contents of education, is one of the formal principles of education. Education is thus committed to neutrality as between its various contents because educa-tion (unlike faith) does not seek to finally make its mind up about its content: the same is true of methods. The methods by which Christianity is taught will be broadly the same as those by which Islam is taught, although perhaps the nature of the content may sometimes lend itself to special methods.[27] But no faith can claim exemption from, for example, the discussion method. To say 'Islam does not ask questions, it simply obeys the Koran', or to say 'Christianity does not offer itself for discussion, but for obedience to the word of God', is irrelevant in determining classroom method. For we are here concerned not with what Christianity or Islam says (except in so far as we are studying the content of those faiths) but with what education says, and with what educational methods demand of those faiths if they are to be treated educationally.

We need then to ask whether there is any sense in which Christianity will retain a 'favoured religion' status in religious education. It would not be acceptable if any such status were to lead to the previous position where Christianity was the religion studied in detail and for the purpose of creating a general sympathy if not a fully formed faith, while the other religions were studied later and only superficially and in order to strengthen the impression in the pupil's mind that Christianity is superior. On the other hand there are certain hard facts about the relationship between Christianity and religious education in this country which cannot be ignored.

Christianity occupies a major segment of the religious phenomena which actually appear in Britain. This is the only religion which is found more or less everywhere. Christianity is also of great significance in that (along with Judaism to a certain extent) it forms and influences any superstitions, beliefs, customs and values which still remain in the popular mentality and way of life and thus Christianity continues to provide whatever rapport there may still be between the people and the overt religious structures. It is for this reason normally the most suitable point at which the significance and role of religion can be explicated. But most importantly of all, the overwhelming proportion of teachers of religion are Christians, often believing and practising. This means that the problem of whether the teaching of world religions (and indeed the problems raised by the whole question of secularization) can commend itself to the Christian conscience is a more vital question for religious education today than the question of whether such teaching can commend itself to the Islamic conscience, although the latter is no different in principle. Christians have no grounds except their numbers upon which to base a claim for special consideration. But numbers cannot be ignored, for in practice power in controlling the trends in religious education is in the hands of Christians and not in the hands of Muslims or Humanists. The responsible use of that power is a major question facing thoughtful Christians in religious education today.

The success of the world religions movement and its effectiveness in further secularizing religious education depends upon Christian teachers and this is why more attention must be given to the problem of helping the Christian teacher to make theological sense of the new syllabuses he is being asked to teach. It is not enough to have an adequate phenomenology of world religions to guide the teacher. We need a more satisfying and coherent Christian theology of that very phenomenology.

There is a third way in which the world religions movement has brought the secularization of religious education to a crisis. This widening of the content of the subject has dealt the death blow to the belief that the teacher himself must be a committed believer in the faith he is teaching. When the Cowper-Temple clause, forbidding denominational distinctiveness, was a living force, the teacher was not permitted to teach many things which he did believe. The fate of the clause is another example of the way in which the Act has been completely overtaken by tendencies within the subject, for it is now realized that it is the distinctive features of denominations and religions which constitute their greatest points of interest and one of their major claims to be studied. But the effect is that the teacher is now expected to teach many things which he positively does not believe or to which he is certainly not committed. So to the secularization of the sponsorship and of the objectives has now been added the secularization (in principle at any rate) of the teaching force. A teacher's own personal faith is now only relevant in so far as it may help or hinder him in the carrying out of his professional tasks. The religious believer is now one of the resources used by the secular religious educator. He may perhaps, if he is careful, use his own religious faith as a resource and he may certainly continue to find in his own faith his motivation for teaching at all (although this is for many teachers the crux of the theological and pastoral problems created by the new trends), but the world religions movement has certainly broken the old alliance between preaching and teaching.

It is clear that these recent trends have destroyed the previous unity between worship, religious education, and the life of the school as a whole. Very few schools can now claim to be Christian communities, if by that is meant a substantial majority of pupils and staff are practising Christians. Even if there were such schools, it is doubtful if it would be appropriate for the county school to adopt such a specific response on a matter which is controversial in our society at large. But whatever the proper stance for the county schools in a country which at least retains some of the outward appearances of being Christian, the actual reactions of pupils during religious education are not much different in the church school from the county school. Even the church school can hardly maintain their integrity as Christian communities, except by reason of the intent of their governing board, often several removes from the realities of daily life in the school.

The task of education is certainly no longer to create Christian discipleship. Religious education is nothing but what education is, within the content area of religion. We have seen how the teaching force itself has in effect been secularized. Religion, like any other subject, can be taught by any well-informed teacher of good will provided that he finds the subject interesting and important. Responsibility for Christian witness in the school rests upon Christian teachers regardless of their subject, and the religion teacher has no obligation whatsoever to be a representative of Christian faith just because he is the religion teacher, but only if he should happen also to be a Christian. When that is the case, as it is in the vast number of cases, the religion teacher must take the utmost care not to allow his enthusiasm for Christianity to overtake his prime Christian duty, which is to be a good educator to his pupils.

With the collapse of the structure, of which it was the apex, school worship is left without support. Worship is inextricably tied to the old sponsoring relationship, since the objects of worship are necessarily those confessed by the religions, and worship proceeds on the assumption that such transcendent realities actually exist and are worthy of worship. It is obvious that in assembly they are held up by the school as objects for worship, not for study. We see then that the two parts of religious education, the assembly and the classroom teaching, have not only drifted apart but have become incompatible; the aims and methods of classroom teaching are no longer compatible with the assumptions of worship.

All of these pressures would be present even if the immigrant communities had not been established in the schools in such numbers. The physical presence of adherents of other faiths has acted as a catalyst, has added urgency, and has created the question of social justice in the treatment of religious education, but no doubt the secularization of the subject would have proceeded in more or less the same way in any case, simply because of the increasing clarification of the concept of education. In schools where there is a sizeable number of members of non-Christian faiths, however, fresh problems certainly arise.

The options confronting the assembly in this multi-religious situation are fairly clear. Assembly could continue to be Christian in the traditional manner and as intended by the Act. Those parents who do not like this can do what they do now — ask for their children to be withdrawn. But when a sufficiently large number is involved, a sort of tip point is reached where this becomes odious and divisive. It might be possible in some cases to arrange for separate assemblies to be held for adherents of various faiths. This would, however, be contrary to the role of assembly and indeed of the county school itself as a cohesive agent in a mixed society. It is also highly probable that if a variety of religious assemblies were to be provided, the question of those who belong to no religion and did not wish to worship anything would become irresistible. Christians, after all, are a minority too. In most cases, the parents of immigrant children of non-Christian faith do not ask for them to be withdrawn. Sometimes this may be because of ignorance of the law (and the school is responsible for this), but usually it is because of a fear of appearing exceptional, or from a desire not to appear disrespectful, or from a desire to come to appreciate the faith of the host country, or through indifference. The presence of religious non-Christians then leads to further complications. If they are there only as spectators the question of the non-religious again becomes acute. Why should they not also be simply spectators? The corporate nature of the worship quickly collapses. If members of non-Christian faiths are present as participators in a Christian act of worship, then either they are being insincere, or (in the case of Islam at least) inconsistent, or they are being confused or subverted. The same comments apply to giving thanks for food 'in the name of our Lord Jesus Christ'. One sometimes sees Sikh, Muslim, Jewish and Hindu children in county primary schools being instructed to utter such words before lunch.

Let us suppose then that the decision is taken, because of the large number of immigrant pupils involved, not to continue with school assembly in a given school as an exclusively Christian act of worship. What then? Again, the alternatives facing the school are equally clear and equally unacceptable. Materials from other faiths could be selected if they were consistent with the Christian faith. This has the advantage of making it possible to go on worshipping, but it has the disadvantage that it may misrepresent the other faiths and it subjects them to a criterion of selection (compatibility with Christianity) which is as humiliating as it is inappropriate. The other alternative is to select from the other faiths those aspects of them which are typical and characteristic of themselves. The advantage is that justice is done to the other faiths, but the disadvantage is that it becomes less and less possible to worship. For worship is the expression of one's total loyalty to certain values; as the values diverge, worship loses its totality, or becomes inconsistent and confused. There remains but one possibility, and that is suggested by the London Agreed Syllabus. 'By adopting a broad definition of worship and linking it imaginatively with life as the pupils know it, it should be possible to achieve a sense of unity within the community, so that excusal for conscientious reasons is minimized, and the boys and girls enabled to appreciate and participate in religious experiences drawn from many sources and traditions.'[28] But how broad can a definition of worship become? How can reason for conscientious withdrawal be minimized except by minimizing doctrinal content? And as doctrinal content is lowered, so is the cognitive aspect of worship. Worship loses its clarity and finally it is without an object. It is then no longer worship of anything. What the London Syllabus is suggesting is that worship should be replaced by a variety of religious ceremonies which would include ingredients from all faiths. This is in some ways a valuable suggestion. But it gives rise to two further questions. Why go on calling such acts worship when they must lack that which is definitive of worship? And secondly, if we are right in regarding the freeing of religious education from ecclesiastical control and sponsorship as being a move towards greater educational validity for the subject, then it is important to insist that religious education, having only just escaped from the clutches of one religion, must not be allowed to fall into the embrace of all of them together. We must continue to affirm that the religions are the phenomena to be studied, and to expect the studious but uncommitted or variously committed to offer worship to the objects of their study is no longer a part of the task of the maintained school. The presence of a variety of religions and non-religious life styles within the school appears thus to be an insuperable obstacle to worship on the part of all the pupils assembled together.

One of the effects of the pluralization of society is that questions previously uncontroversial become controversial. We have already seen that the best path for the county school in a pluralistic society is to teach nothing, to present nothing as if it were necessarily true, as if it were assumed to be true, as if the school as school had adopted an official position towards it.

But that is exactly what necessarily takes place in school assembly. The school *qua* school led by its chief officials in company requires its pupils to worship the Christian God.[29]

Religion is, of course, not the only controversial subject. History, social studies, current affairs, indeed almost any subject if taught in a lively and life-related manner, will give rise to controversy. For the school to pretend that this controversy does not exist or to present to its pupils an artificial unanimity of staff opinion on religious matters is to deny its role as an educational institution.

Of all aspects of religious education, worship is most difficult to defend against the charge of indoctrination. In the widely read writings of Canon J.G. Williams, neglect of educational ethics is elevated into an argument for school worship. The peculiar problems of worship in the county

schools arise, it is claimed, from the fact that worship does
not even begin 'to be possible outside the provision which
God has made within the sacramental life of his Church'.[30]
The answer suggested by Williams is that the school should be
made as much like the church as possible. Hence 'in school
worship the claims of the Church must always be kept clearly
in sight'.[31] No attempt is made to work out any independent
justification for the state teaching of religion, and the
discussion concludes that 'until our educational system is
once again . . . inspired by a theological outlook that gives
unity and coherence to the whole field, we must continue to
look to the Church school as the one place where education
can be, in the Christian sense, complete'.[32] But if this is so,
Christian parents are conscience bound, as indeed Roman
Catholic policy still suggests, to withdraw their children from
the state system and to place them in church schools.

But the most disturbing feature of the treatment of state
school worship in this book is that it is frankly regarded as a
powerful means of instilling religious doctrine. ' . . . it is
because in worship these attributes of God are simply taken
for granted, and not argued or deliberately taught, that
worship is the most powerful medium of all for communicating dogmatic truth. It is far more powerful than the direct
instruction of the classroom, simply because it teaches
incidentally and by implication; and it is the things which are
taken for granted, the implicit assumptions, rather than any
kind of explicit teaching, that sink most deeply into the
subconscious mind and become the foundations of
"faith".'[33] Indoctrination is regarded by Williams as being
evil when it destroys the freedom and responsibility of the
pupil,[34] but this is surely just what he regards as being most
valuable about assembly. It is effective precisely for this reason
because it deprives the pupil of his responsibility. He does not
know what is going on as the dogmatic truths sink most
deeply into his subconscious mind to become foundations
for 'faith'.

Williams rightly regards the communication and reinforcement of its cognitive assumptions as being inseparable from
any act of worship. Now if an adult, knowing that this is so,
engages with his peers in an act of worship, knowing that at a
level deeper than the rational, the rational choice he has

already made will be strengthened, this is entirely legitimate and the adult believer does so on his own responsibility. But if (as is the case in Williams' argument) worship is recommended because of its potency for influencing[35] by deliberately non-rational means the uncommitted young person, who has no choice but to be there, and does not know what is happening to him, such worship must be regarded as uneducational and un-Christian. Of course, very often the young person knows only too well what is being done to him. He resists it with contempt. Such aggressively nurturing procedures are then discredited not only as attempted indoctrination, but as failing in this very attempt. This double disgrace is one of the worst features of religious education and one of the most prominent reasons for the failure of Christian nurture in the state school.

There have been several atempts in recent years to justify school worship on educational grounds. The most influential of these was that contained in *The Fourth R* (The Durham Report) in 1970. A number of arguments are offered in defence of school worship, but the one derived from consideration of educational ideals is 'the one most cogent reason why school worship must remain in English schools'.[36] Two related arguments may be discerned. The first deals with the content of religious education and the second deals with the aims of religious education. The argument from content may be summarized as follows:

1. Religion is educationally justifiable as part of the curriculum in the county schools.[37]
2. Worship is a 'significant feature'[38] of religion.
3. 'Some experience of worship is essential . . . if justice is to be done to the content of religious education.'[39]

The first proposition certainly needs qualification and is indeed qualified both directly and by implication at various points in the Report. The overall position in the Report seems to be the more modest one that some aspects of some religions are justifiable as part of the curriculum. It is indicated, for example, that the doctrine of original sin, in some of its various forms, is not a suitable basis for the upbringing of children but that the concept of Christian love is highly significant for the whole of the educational process.[40] Certain parts of the Old Testament, the Report suggests, could inhibit moral development,[41] so these parts of the religious literature could hardly be justified within the school curriculum. We are even given a criterion for the selection of a suitable religion for the curriculum: a religion with an exploratory approach towards its own theology is more consistent with modern educational requirements in the West than a religion with a closed and static theology.[42] The teacher obviously must make a selection from numerous sacred books[43] and must go on selecting from the immense quantity of religious facts and beliefs those which he finds most appropriate to his pupils and most consistent with the ethos of the educational environment within which he works. So he asks if the proposed material is pupil-related, if it is relevant, and if it can be taught in an open-ended way.[44] We conclude that the general intention of the Report is to suggest that there are aspects of a particular religion or of religion in general which, however significant they may be in their native religious habitat, might not necessarily be studied in the county school or in any school, perhaps because the material is beyond the understanding of the pupils or perhaps because the material is unhappy in its association with the ideals of the rest of the curriculum.

Now this qualifying of the first proposition leads to some comments about the second one. Worship is indeed a significant feature of the Christian religion and of most religions, but this in itself does not permit us to include either the study or the practice of worship in the curriculum. Only if there were no over-riding objections to its inclusion (such as the examples mentioned in the last paragraph) would the claim that a certain item is necessary in order to do full justice to a subject be a strong one. Private prayer is rather a significant feature of Christianity, and so is the idea and practice of the mission of the church in evangelism, but teachers in county schools do not set so many minutes of private prayer as homework nor a certain amount of missioning experience as a vacation task. On the other hand, service to others, which is also an essential aspect of Christianity, is encouraged for all pupils by most religion teachers (and others) and often officially supported by schools. Some important features of Christianity, such as participation in the Eucharist, are not insisted on in county schools partly for ecclesiastical reasons, and others like prayer in private and having missioning experience are not insisted upon mainly for educational reasons. So we see that the school, for several reasons, is discriminating between aspects of the Christian faith, although all aspects might be thought equally vital to the Christian faith itself. These examples may serve to illustrate the point that although certain important aspects of religion ought to be included we cannot claim, as the Report does, that any given aspect must be studied or performed in school simply because without it the subject will be incomplete. We can only make this claim if there are no over-riding considerations. There are such over-riding considerations in the case of performing worship in school assembly but not in the case of studying worship.

We next consider the argument from the aim of religious education, which appears at several points in the Report. It may be summarized as follows.

1. The aims of religious education may be educationally justified.[45]

2. Experience of worship is a necessary stage in the fulfilment of these aims: (*a*) the linguistic argument: to understand a religious proposition it is necessary to see it in its real-life setting; this setting includes the ritualistic and worshipful contexts of religious statements[46]; (*b*) the experiential argument: worship is the practical application, the experienced reality of religion, corresponding to the practical aspects of other subjects.[47] Thus putting (*a*) and (*b*) together, the Report concludes that 'religious understanding' (one of the acceptable aims of religious education) 'cannot be developed without experience of worship'.

3. Acceptance of the aims of religious education entails acceptance of regular school worship.

The linguistic argument, as it is here being called, is in itself a valuable comment on teaching religion. It is undoubtedly true that religious statements cannot be correctly understood if they are removed from the contexts in which religious communities use them. The devotional and liturgical settings are amongst the most important and certainly these settings and the language used should be studied. But there does not seem sufficient reason for thinking (as the Report appears to) that this understanding can only come or may best come through the pupil's actual participation as a worshipper in regular services of worship at school.

Religious educators want their pupils to exercise empathy towards religious people and critical sympathy towards what they say. They rightly want them to understand, as far as the limits of the county school situation permit, what it feels like to be religious. Since it is not the object of teachers of religion to secure or even 'to press for acceptance of a particular faith or belief system'[48] it is not legitimate to have pupils acquire an understanding of what it feels like to be a Christian by actually converting them, getting them to pray or to take part in the sacraments. The task must therefore be done by good teaching, by representation, by imagination and by the growth of insight. It may be done by meeting, listening to and talking with religious believers, by collecting their prayers, and by visiting and observing (whether on or off the school premises) religious worship and seeking to comprehend the intentions of such services. But the need to study the worshipful context of religious language does not seem to require actual pupil worship, even if the number of school services is reduced from five to two or three a week.[49] There are, in short, various ways in which one can 'look to the worshipping activities'[50] and taking part in official school services is in some ways the least desirable.

The experiential argument, as it is here being called, is not satisfactory for a number of reasons. Worship is not the only or the main way the pupils actually experience religion and it does not therefore correspond to the practical aspects of other subjects. In the case of religious studies, the immediately experienced aspects include sensing the impact of great lives, following a religious discussion between teacher and class, seeing how a teacher deals with a religious problem, painting or acting religious scenes or portraying religious emotions or watching and (as uncommitted guests) courteously taking part in the ceremonies of various religious groups. There is a further sense in which all experience of service, of love, of alienation and of reconciliation may, as the Report shows so clearly, help the pupil existentially to understand certain religious expressions and symbols. It is misleading to narrow this wide range of ways in which pupils may be helped to experience the power of religion to their actual participation in school worship. The error rests upon the supposition that in. the classroom one is only talking about religion, whereas in worship one is actually approaching God. But we ought to say instead that experiencing worship is but one of the ways in which pupils may come to understand what it would be like if they believed in God and what it means to claim that there is a God to believe in. We should then ask whether some of the ways are educationally preferable to other ways.

We have already seen, and the Report rightly emphasizes, that teachers of religion may not seek to convert them nor may they expose them exclusively to one religion in the hope that they will come to accept that one, nor may they take advantage of their superior knowledge and perhaps superior intelligence to force their own or somebody else's religious views on their pupils. Just as some content of religion is suitable for schools and some is not, so some means of introducing religion are legitimate and others are not. Expecting, indeed requiring pupils to worship God, seems to be in the latter category.

The arguments which the Report advances to show that school worship is *required* by educational considerations cannot be sustained. Not only do these arguments fail to compel the conclusion, but other difficulties arise and are considered in the Report which count rather strongly against the conclusion.

The Report discusses the tensions which exist between worship understood theologically and worship understood educationally.

The central purpose of Christian worship is 'to respond appropriately to the love and grace of God as seen in Jesus Christ, and to make the divine power a reality in the lives of the worshippers'.[51] But then in discussing the educational use to which worship is put in the schools, the Report reminds us forcefully: 'It can only be worship if it is indeed the appropriate response of creature to creator and, as such, an activity to be undertaken for its own sake.'[52] The problem which immediately arises is faced in what follows.

'To regard it in this way is admittedly, and as the secularist maintains, to assume the truth of certain Christian doctrines.'[53]

But while worship assumes the truth, religious education, the Report rightly points out, must be heuristic: ' . . . the exploratory aspects of a discipline whose task of interpretation is never complete nor rounded off in a neat system'.[54] ' . . . religious education is conducted in the form of an exploration, that no one view point is considered automatically or regarded as invariably correct.'[55] The Report is well aware then of the tension between worship which, since it assumes the truth of certain doctrines appears to be a closed intellectual activity, and the rest of religious education where no doctrine or truth is considered invariably correct.

This problem is dealt with in the Report in two ways. The first involves a consideration of the psychology of the worshipper. The theological point of view, it is suggested, does not exhaust the description of worship. If held too exclusively a theological description may be 'too restrictive'[56] and worship 'cannot solely be defined' in this way. Worship has 'diverse origins' and produces a 'diversity of human reactions'.[57] When we contemplate the psychological responses to any given act of worship or examine the composition of almost any worshipping group, it can be seen that 'attendance at an act of worship does not necessarily imply or presuppose total personal commitment to the object of worship'.[58] This point is supported by an analysis of worship into the expressive function and the didactic. 'Needs and fears' may be expressed in worship as well as adoration, and worship shares with classroom activity a certain teaching function.[59]

These replies hardly meet the force of the problem of the tension between worship and education. Although not exhaustive, the theological description of worship is, as the Report rightly emphasizes,[60] essential for Christians and a consideration of the variety of moods and reactions of those present at an act of worship in no way weakens the demand made by the theological nature of the act. To what extent, then, does the observation that people vary in their reactions to worship offer relief to the conscience of the uncommitted person? For although it is valuable to respond with 'humility and awe' or with 'world-weariness and fear',[61] is it also valuable to respond with scepticism, or with unqualified disbelief, and with rejection of the assumptions of worship? Attendance may not imply total commitment, but does it imply any commitment at all? It might be said that all it need imply is commitment to a search for religious truth. Worship, however, assumes certain doctrines to be true. There is considerable difference between a search for truth and an assumption of truth.[62]

Moreover, members of staff and pupils are usually not only expected or required (as the case may be) to attend. They are expected or required to take part. They hold hymn books in their hands. They bow their heads. They stand or sit together at the same times. They sing and speak words addressed to God and to Jesus Christ. School worship is almost never conceived of as being presented by the religious education department or the headteacher to mere spectators. The act of worship in schools assumes participation, and those who do not wish to offer worship to Christ withdraw. And those who participate in the worship participate in fact or by strong implication in the assumptions upon which the worship is based and which it exists to express.[63]

As for the division of worship into expressive and didactic functions, this is inadequate since the most significant function of worship is omitted, namely the affirmative. As for the didactic function of worship, it is fundamentally different from that which takes place in the classroom. Worship cannot be open; classroom teaching in religion must be open.

Openness, the Report indicates, does not mean that the teaching of religion will proceed without any basic assumptions.[64] But no basic assumption is free from examination and criticism at some time or other in the teaching periods. One cannot be always discussing the existence of God; sometimes one must proceed on the assumption that there is (or is not) a God and see what may follow. Next week, this assumption will itself be looked at. In worship, however, one not only starts by assuming the truth of certain doctrines, one finishes in exactly the same way.[65]

The secularization of religious education has thus driven a wedge between the assembly and the classroom. This is not because assembly has changed. In fact, religious education at this point presents us with another paradox. Worship is not controlled in the Act as to its content, yet it has remained much the same. Classroom work is strictly controlled, yet it has changed. The Agreed Syllabuses control the content of classroom work in a manner which has no parallel in other school subjects. Yet when we read the syllabuses of the last four or five years and compare them with those produced during the forties we see that the subject has, in spite of the cumbersome and archaic machinery required to set it in operation, undergone processes of curriculum development not unlike those taking place in other subjects. The Agreed Syllabuses when good have inspired new approaches; when less satisfactory they have acted as a challenge and an irritant. The content of worship, however, is not defined in the Act. We are told what worship must not be. It must not contain formularies or catechisms distinctive of a particular denomination. But we are not told what worship must be, subject to this particular restriction. Schools were always completely free to devise such forms of worship as they thought fit. And yet worship has resisted change more successfully than any other part of the school curriculum. The service books used are often volumes which the headmaster picked up in the study of his retired predecessor. They will often be books published in the fifties and will even then be later editions or impressions of works originally compiled in the thirties or earlier.

Perhaps it would have been good if as well as Agreed Syllabuses of classroom work, we have had Agreed Syllabuses of school assembly. That, however, was psychologically impossible. Worship (although it was often expected that children would learn something from it) was never subjected to the same scrutiny as the rest of the educational work of the school. It was indeed not thought of as education but as worship, which is what it was intended to be.[66] So one needed not a lesson plan but a lectionary, not a syllabus but a service book. Teachers were not accustomed to ask after assembly: 'What have our pupils learned this morning? What was new to them? How does it fit into work being done elsewhere? Is there any way we can help them to understand that better if we do it again some other time? Was it understandable to both younger and older pupils?' It is symptomatic of the situation that as long as hymns and prayers and Bible readings are used, the question of comprehension by various age groups rarely arises, but as soon as one asks about the educational role of assembly such questions arise in an important way.

What is the reason for the conservatism of school assembly? How has it managed to resist change so successfully? In the first place, as we have seen, assembly has occupied a place of immunity from educational scrutiny. Secondly, religion on the whole is a conservative force in society, and liturgy is the most conservative aspect of religious tradition. In the third place, many schools have been quite at a loss to know what to do about it, and although perplexed and dissatisfied, have not been able to reach agreement about any changes. But probably the most important factor in preserving worship relatively unchanged, particularly in the secondary schools, has been its role as the major means whereby the school hierarchy is exhibited and reinforced. The myths and rituals of ancient Israel served to support sacred kingship; in modern Britain they serve to support sacred headship. The assembly is the main forum through which the headmaster exercises his personality and his authority directly upon the school. The prefects usher pupils in, form by form, row by row, the head prefect calls for silence, the staff file on to the stage or to raised chairs at the back of the hall; finally the head himself enters in an atmosphere of complete silence. One man stands while six hundred heads are bowed. The worship is followed by admonitions and exhortations. Notices are read and sports results announced. The role of the assembly in discipline and control is typified by what is perhaps the most common context in which assembly is referred to in the every-day life of the school: 'I'll grab him coming out of assembly.'[6][7] The actual form and content of the worship often express the same function. In many schools the order of persons who read the lesson follows the order of the hierarchy. The head reads on the first day of term, the deputy and the house masters on following days, then the staff in order of seniority, the head of the school followed by the prefects and finally the form captains from the science sixth down to 1d.

This practice is dying out rapidly but still exists and was not uncommon particularly in boys secondary schools a few years ago. We have already seen how often the prayers were based around the virtues and the vices most favoured and despised by school teachers in pupils.

The effect of all this upon the religious attitudes of young people is rather negative. God is seen as the God of the adult, of the school teacher.[68] He is God the Judge, the Lord, the God of Law and Order. School assembly can be thought of as an institutional form of child control through coalition with God.[69] One begins to ask whether religious education, already not one of the strong subjects of the curriculum, can afford the alliance with school assembly.

To complete our survey of the problems facing school worship we must look at it against the backdrop of spirituality today. Worship is under close scrutiny throughout the Christian communities in the Western world, to go no further afield. Declining attendances at traditional public worship are found side by side with the appearance of new forms of worship. Habits of prayer and family devotion are undergoing extensive change within Christian churches, some forms of spirituality taking the shape of activism, others emerging in the charismatic movements. It would be odd if worship and spirituality, undergoing such evolution within religious groups, were not to be under some strain in the much more exposed situation in the secondary school. As new forms of youthful spirituality are created, teachers are increasingly in danger of offering to young people patterns of devotion which mean less and less to anyone.

Do the questions asked in this chapter have relevance to the infant and junior school? Reference has been made to the manner in which the conduct of school worship expects or requires young people to confess or associate themselves with the confession of a faith they may not and often do not hold. Since to hold or refuse to hold a faith requires some understanding of the issues involved, it might be thought that young children were not capable of either holding or rejecting a religious faith and that therefore there could be no objection against requiring them to go through the motions. It is not possible, it might be thought, for a child to worship contrary to his own conscience since (unlike the adolescent) he has not the maturity to judge that he rejects the cognitions involved in the worship.

It is admittedly more difficult for the teacher of younger children to handle controversial subjects in the proper way. The object of the school must be at least in part to accustom children to the idea that adults do have different ideas about various subjects. This should be brought home to the child as soon as possible, which means as soon as the child is capable of appreciating the existence of disagreement without being unduly distressed. Although they cannot appreciate the metaphysical theology of belief in God, children of nine and ten can understand very well that adults have different ideas about God and children of that age will sometimes affirm or deny belief in God.

Now one of the questions to ask about assembly in the junior and infant school is whether it hastens the day of this readiness for the appreciation of different points of view, or whether it defers it by presenting to the child an alleged unanimity. Is the intention to widen the options in front of the child by preparing him to face the choices of adolescence or is the intention rather to narrow the options for the child by establishing him in one faith and outlook?

It is certainly one of the important tasks of schools, whether for younger or older pupils, to show that there is more than one way of living and believing. In so far as religious ways of life have been and continue to be one of the major possibilities, schools should continue to help young people to see that life may be lived in a religious way. This is an argument for religious education and for the inclusion of some understanding of worship and spirituality in religion syllabuses, and if religion becomes increasingly part of the counter culture, and is perhaps increasingly neglected in the homes of many young people, the duty of the school to make these broadening provisions will increase.

But none of these reflections justifies the county primary school in adopting an official position towards the Christian faith, or towards humanism or communism or Islam or any of the other options found in this country today. An assembly which indicates such a sustained and unilateral official commitment would be as uneducational in the primary school as it would be in the technical college.

5   *Worship in the Church Schools*

In chapters 2 and 3 we have been concerned with the county schools. It has been argued that because of the changes in religious education in the county schools, because of the pluralistic nature of the school communities and of the community at large to which the school is responsible, because of the nature of the education process compared with the nature of worship, and so on, that worship in the county school is an anomaly. We now have the difficult task of determining to what extent these considerations apply also to the church schools.

The extent to which church schools can be considered Christian communities varies greatly. There are schools, such as some of the schools set up by independent groups of evangelical Protestants and those provided by some of the Roman Catholic teaching orders, which can be considered as much a part of the Christian community as the congregation which meets for worship on Sunday. There may be some Catholic parochial schools where all the children in attendance are baptized children of Christian parents who themselves support the school financially. Schools such as these do not offer us the problems of plurality which the county schools do, and they are not public property but church property. In schools such as these, the unity of the philosophy of Christian education which prevailed in the county schools from about 1920 to 1965 is still unbroken. Worship is not isolated from religious education and from the rest of the curriculum; it still expresses the objectives of the schools which can be such limited objectives because the schools are part of a limited and a specific society, the Christian church. The existence of such schools remains a

significant expression of parental rights regarding the upbringing of their own children.

We have discussed the relationship between worship and
education in chapter 3, showing that although different in
their assumptions and attitudes, and consequently in some
degree of tension, worship and education may be compatible
since they are both ultimately fed by the same Christian
faith, which is a necessary base for worship and a possible
base for education. It is not inconsistent, therefore, for the
same individual to worship sometimes and to educate or be
educated at other times, and we have discussed the various
kinds of risks which each activity poses for the other, as well
as the risks created when one activity is carried on without
the other. It is only the distinctive nature of the state school
in the pluralistic society, within a curriculum which is no
longer based on a Christian philosophy, containing a religious
education which has become secularized, that creates the
situation in which worship becomes anomalous. It would be
quite consistent (although risky) for a congregation worshipping on Sunday to embark on a programme of education for
itself and its children and it would be quite proper for a day
school which genuinely represents a Christian community in
that it is owned, maintained, staffed and attended by
Christians and children of Christians to embark on a
programme of worship. Whether it would be not only proper
but advisable would be a matter for the school and its
supporters to decide.

Does the tension between worship and religious education
not apply in the Christian school? The tension only becomes
an incompatibility in the case of the state school, which has
no right to be closed on controversial religious matters. The
tension is greater between worship and a religious general
education which contains specific education but no nurture
than it is between worship and a religious general education
which contains nurture as well as specific education. Christian schools may rightfully intend to nurture in the Christian
faith as well as to educate specifically. This nurturing
function provides a bridge between specific education and
worship, a bridge which in the state school is lacking.

Is school worship then less indoctrinatory in church
schools than in state schools? Indoctrination is an attempt to

implant conviction without gaining the consent of the reason. (We can see that indoctrination is an illogical activity, since to be convinced *means* to be persuaded by the arguments.) But let us suppose that the communication is directed towards people who are already convinced by the arguments and are committed to faith in Christianity. It has been observed that it is not improper for a believing adult, knowing that worship will deepen his faith in ways which are different from the rational, voluntarily to engage in worship with his fellow believers. The unethical aspect of indoctrination lies in its intention to deprive the hearer of his reason. But, the claims of reason having been met, there is nothing wrong with surrendering oneself to emotion. There is a difference, then, between the situation where, the claims of reason having been met, I surrender myself to emotion, and the situation where I am subjected to emotion and repetition *in order to prevent* me from thinking. In the first situation, I suspend my reason; in the second situation, my reason is taken from me without my knowledge or consent.

The crux of the situation in school is thus whether school worship is intended to be a way of influencing the uncommitted. It is wrong in the state school because of the fact that the state school (in all but a few rural areas) is no longer a Christian community and contains many young people who are uncommitted. But if the congregation worshipping in the school assembly were as much a part of the church as the congregation which gathered for worship on Sunday in the church building, then no attempt would be made to influence the uncommitted.

But now we must distinguish between the worship of students in a theological college and worship of boys and girls in a church primary school. The theological students are adults, gathered voluntarily to express their faith in a ritual of words, music and action which transcends reason. They themselves take responsibility for the effect of worship upon them, and since their reason is already engaged, the effect of their worship should be to integrate them yet more deeply in harmony with faith. Children, however, are not in school voluntarily, or are not of an age to exercise choice about such a matter. We remind ourselves now of the discussion of the church's responsibility in the provision of worship for its own baptized children. If children cannot comprehend the beliefs associated with worship, they can only be expected to worship in an attenuated sense. What will be provided for them will to that extent be pre-worship.

We must now return to the distinctions between nurture, indoctrination and specific education. The borders between these activities, which seemed reasonably clear in chapter 1, seem in danger of collapsing. The church nurtures its children in doctrines of the faith as well as in character and in the qualities of the religious life. What is the difference between such nurture and indoctrination?

A child is nurtured in the tradition into which the circumstances of his birth have thrown him. But he is indoctrinated into an alien way of life. His nurture is a prolonging of the conditions of his infancy. He is nurtured physically and psychologically by his parents, growing into their social, political and religious forms of life without realizing at first that there is anything else. The parents who gave him physical existence will give him speech, human relationships and the whole structure of their culture (a good deal of which they themselves may not realize is local and distinctive) including their religious outlooks and customs. No parent should feel hesitant about this. It is part of being a parent, of nurturing a social being, of establishing humanity.

But if the parents desire not only to nurture, to protect, to allow growth, but also to determine the totality of their child's life for ever, if they do not make nurture a preparation for specific education, if they intend always to keep their child from responsible choice, then they are on the way towards indoctrination. Nurture seeks to bring up a Christian child to be a Christian adult never having *known* himself as anything other;[1] it does not seek to bring him up never having *imagined* himself as being anything other, and therefore *incapable* of being anything other. If nurture did that, it would not only pass on the past to the child, it would create the future for the child. It would intend not only to start the child but to finish him. And a nurture which claims to be able to finish the personhood of the child, to complete his humanity, has betrayed the image of man. For if nurture claims to finish a person, it claims to know what the finished person will be. So the integrity, the uniqueness of that person is denied. The parents ought not to deprive the child of his own vocation, of the possibility of achieving his own humanity. Humanity must be achieved, as well as received. This then is a fundamental question for Christian parents and for church schools: is the child being nurtured into person-hood by encouraging him to enter fully into his 'given' inheritance, to explore it, and finally to see it in contrast to other possibilities? Or is the nurture depriving him of his personhood by presuming to know what that personhood will be and simply presenting him with it? Is the tradition the womb or the straitjacket? This is the difference between nurture and indoctrination: if the child is brought up within the circumstances and traditions of his birth in such a way as to limit and even control his future by making it impossible for him to escape his past, he is indoctrinated; if a child is brought up in an alien tradition in circumstances which are not those of his heritage, then his past is taken from him. If this is done so as to keep him for ever in that alien tradition, he is deprived of his past and his future as well; then also he is indoctrinated. But if he is brought up in his native tradition in such a way as to enter into dialogue with it, to become aware of it, so that he may appropriate it or he may reject it, then he has been nurtured in the Christian way.

But what is the distinction between such nurture and specific education? For both are characterized by openness. And the openness has the same source in the historical (thus unpredictable) nature of Christian faith. The differences are:

1. Children can be educated into many religions but only nurtured into one — that of their family circumstances. Christian nurture is thus only appropriate for those from Christian families; education is appropriate for all.

2. The teacher who nurtures and the teacher who educates have different hopes: the nurturer hopes the child will confirm his religious tradition in rational choice; the educator cannot hope this — or if he has the hope, he must not do anything about it — firstly because he may not be dealing with children who have any religious tradition and in that case, if he gives expression to such a hope he would not be an educator any longer but an evangelist and secondly because education is not concerned to win the assent of the

pupil towards its content.

3. In nurture the Christian theological basis of the openness is explicit; in education it is implicit. Only the believer can nurture, but the educator need not be a believer.

4. Nurture is a domestic activity of the church; education is a public activity of the pluralist society.

5. The relation between nurture and education is a little bit like the relation between theology and philosophy. The latter are both critical, open, rational activities, but theology is faith in quest of reason, or reason in defence of faith, whereas in philosophy reason knows no quest but for itself and defends only its own purity. So nurture is a servant of faith; education (although like philosophy it may owe much to faith and may be harmonious with faith) has no aim but to make further enquiry possible.

Let us return to the question of nurture in the truly Christian schools. Such nurture is, we conclude, perfectly proper. But, we have asked, is it advisable? Within what limits may it be conducted? For, although they are Christian schools, we are still speaking of schools. These Christian schools still ought to be, and claim to be, offering an education which includes specific education. Gabriel Moran has pointed out [2] that in the days before the modern conception of education arose, what the church did was the same as what everyone else did; indeed, in medieval Europe, there was nobody else. Now, however, there is a possibility that what the church does by way of education will be more and more different from what everybody else acknowledges as being education, or (to put it in our own terms), that the general education of the church will lack the ingredient of specific education. We conclude from this that although Christian schools may offer nurture to their pupils and this may take the form of worship and catechizing, they may not neglect to specifically educate their pupils as well, and particularly in the field of religion. There will certainly be groups of Christians who in the name of education and parents' rights will continue to maintain schools which will be islands of protective nurture and which will not in fact attempt to offer a critical, descriptive education into religion. Such schools will be increasingly exposed as not being educational establishments.

The status of most church schools is, however, more ambiguous than the ones so far described. In England and Wales most church schools also have a relationship to the state and are in receipt of state aid. They have controlled or aided status, or they may be direct grant or special agreement schools. They draw on catchment areas which are often indistinguishable from those of the county schools. They may have entrance requirements, but these will often be of an academic not a religious nature, although preference may be given to the children of church-going parents. The motivation of the parents is often social and academic rather than religious. The staff in the non-Catholic aided and certainly in the controlled schools consists of Christians and non-Christians often in comparable proportions to the staff of a county school.

Questions about the function of these voluntary aided and controlled schools are increasingly asked and are not easy to answer. If the church schools are intended to be a service to the community by offering education just as the church hospitals offer healing, then we would need to ask even more urgently than at present whether the church's limited resources are being utilized to the greatest advantage by the provision of schools. On the other hand, the church schools may be intended to serve the church and thus to provide Christian nurture and evangelism. These aims are legitimate, as we have seen, provided that they are a supplement to and not a substitute for the education which must be the prime purpose of a school. It seems to follow then that church schools of all types and degrees may offer nurture. Indeed, they have a duty to offer nurture. But they have no right to compel pupils to be nurtured, or to insist that they attend and take part in nurturing occasions. Pupils (and their parents) in church schools have a right to expect that the authorities in the school will provide a chapel and a chaplain and other aids for coming to know and live and worship as Christians. But because of the mixed nature of most church schools and because of the educational role of all of them, nurture must be offered, not enforced. Worship is necessarily a nurturing activity. It must be available but it must not be compulsory.

The tragedy of many of the church schools, particularly the so-called 'public' and independent schools, is that they have neither nurtured nor educated in religion. They have not nurtured because they have not been able to maintain a sufficiently distinctive staff and clientele and their ethos has not been sufficiently distinctive of Christian faith. Although they profess their religious interest as one of their major claims to distinct existence, close examination often indicates that they make little serious effort to educate into religion. The chaplain is sometimes the only specialist not trained as a teacher, his is the only department without a specialist room and without adequate timetabling arrangements. With neither a thorough education nor an effective nurture into Christian faith many of these schools fall between two stools. Religion in them then serves quite different and less creditable functions. Compulsory chapel must be maintained because if it went, the next thing to go would be compulsory army cadets.

Whatever its other functions, the church school is part of the church's mission to education. The church may nurture those of its members who work in industry and may evangelize others in industry. But when we ask about the church's mission to the structures and processes of industry, our reply will not be in terms of explicit Christian nurture but of justice, concern for the environment and so on. Similarly, when we ask about the mission of the church to educational processes and structures, we will not reply only in terms of Christian nurture and evangelism but in terms of freedom, growth and social change as effected by education. One of the less attractive results of the formation and support of the church schools is that they tend to provide an alibi for the churches, who are tempted to think that their responsibility to education is discharged if they maintain a school, particularly if it is 'well known'.

We may conclude that in institutions, whether church or state, in which an educational purpose predominates, pupils cannot be treated as if they have reached the end of a process into which it is the purpose of the institution to initiate them.

However, with these reservations, in church schools it will be proper to continue to offer worship.[3] It seems appropriate then to reflect on the forms and style of the worship to be presented. The traditional medium of Protestant worship is the spoken (or sung) word, either extempore or read. The children's talk delivered on Sunday morning by the minister is a typical degeneration of this over-emphasis on speaking. The hostility of the Protestant tradition towards other media is due to many factors which cannot be unravelled now but which include a failure to distinguish between idols and icons, an ambiguous attitude towards nature and the body justified by an extreme doctrine of the fall, the rejection of the feminine, and an over-rational approach towards religion, typified by activities such as reading and the high value placed upon independent judgment and discursive preaching. The emphasis upon the word, while one of the glories of Protestantism, has too often obscured the incarnation of the word. John 1.14 is the key to a theology of the media and of their use in worship. Diversification of the media is one of the keys to the recovery of worship in the Christian school.

Any attempt to depart from exclusively verbal worship seems gimmicky to some people. A gimmick is an attention-catching device which has no inner relation in content or purpose to the thing to which it draws attention. It would be a mistake to confuse innovation with gimmickry. This is the mistake of the traditionalist. Gimmickry, on the other hand, is the error of the enthusiast who wants to communicate but lacks the guidance of a theory (and particularly a theology) of religious education.

We must distinguish not only between gimmickry and innovation but also between innovation and experiment in worship. If by experimental worship all that is meant is that the worship is tentative and cast in a temporary form, the word 'experimental' may be helpful. But it sometimes suggests that we have fixed concepts which we wish to convey or certain emotions which we wish to evoke and that we manipulate the variables in order to see whether a new method might work. This is not an acceptable sense of 'experimental'. Either we experiment upon our pupils or upon ourselves. Both possibilities suggest a degree of artificiality and calculation which is foreign to the spirit of worship. God is worshipped in new ways not because we wish to experiment but because we are new people in a new age. We have our wine in new skins not because they look better than the old and might sell more wine, but because the wine itself is new.

To begin to think about the use of various media in worship, we need to think about the senses themselves and what each has to contribute. Let us compare the ear with the eye. The sense of sight has to be extended into allegory before it can describe the relationship between God and man. 'The Lord sees not as man sees; man looks on the outward appearance, but the Lord looks on the heart.'[4] Sight is to do with the outward, with surfaces. But hearing perceives internal structures. Hearing links together the interiors of subjects, whereas seeing links the exteriors of objects. Christ is thus described as the word of God, springing from the Father's bosom and making him known. The lie, the false speech, makes it impossible to penetrate the heart and thus the lie shuts off the inner man. To reduce hearing to seeing is 'hardening of the heart', since the word which enters into the heart is rejected and only the outer appearance is in obedience to God.

Music speaks to the interior. Like glossolalia and the essence of prayer which is the unutterable groaning of the spirit, music transcends speech. When we are taken from the babel of tongues which is the confusion of many languages, to the unity of the pentecostal tongues, then language is transcended by divine sound. Sound itself is pre-rational; but music is post-rational. It is the post-rationality which gives music its power to be both more sublime and more superficial than the spoken word. Post rationality means that music, unlike mere sound and the noises of nature, expresses an intention announced in a form. It is the form of music (its architecture, its harmonic, rhythmic and tonic shape) which is significant in meditation rather than its content (the subject of the music, its theme, whether expressed in words or in programmatic notes). It is the form of a late Beethoven quartet which draws the solitary listener into meditative introspection, and the repetition of controlled monotonous phrases in chanting creates the atmosphere of group concentration which prepares for communal meditation.

Unlike the ear, the eye sets objects out in space thus exhibiting relationships between the position of things. This, plus the power of sight to concentrate on one part of the field, makes it possible to pay attention to one part of a picture and then move on to another without losing the relationship between the two. This can be done by the ear, as for example when you listen to the first violin or the flute, but it requires effort. The ear is not a discriminatory sense organ in the way the eye is, as can be realized by the fact that even the trained ear can only simultaneously distinguish a handful of sounds while the eye can hold in relationship hundreds of parts when, for example, it looks at a pattern. Art also has a conceptual power of a different sort from music. Highly abstract art is an attempt to reach greater conceptual purity. This capacity to present new concepts and new relationships between them is part of the meditative power of art. In art, time is suspended; one can wander around inside a picture returning at will to this or that aspect of it. Music, like speech, is encapsulated within time; it travels onwards perpetually. Music, however, springs from silence and prepares for silence just as a picture prepares for either darkness or unbroken light. Darkness, light and silence are the centre of meditation and worship; art and music are the thresholds.

With art as with music, form is more important in meditation than content. Paul Tillich's theory of symbols which illuminates the conduct of school worship includes the point that a symbol must be broken to become transparent to its depth, i.e. that towards which it points, that of which it is symbolic.[5] This power of a picture to point beyond itself is an aspect of its technique, its form, or (we might say) its spirit. The actual subject, while not without importance, is not the crucial aspect of a picture when it is being considered as an aid to meditation.

This can be seen clearly in the case of biblical art. The question is whether the picture literalizes the subject or symbolizes it. To literalize a subject is to profess to answer the question: what was it like at the time? To symbolize a subject is to talk about the divine reality of which it is the revelation. When a picture of a biblical event is treated in this symbolic manner, it may become revelatory as the original event was revelatory. As it represents the revelation, it lifts the observer into the power of the divine. Only the symbolic picture is suitable for use in worship. But sometimes the most valuable art for use in meditation is art done by the worshipper himself, for then the event, its symbolic meaning, and his own inner life are already fused in the picture. In meditation he lives again the creative moment of its emergence. One can also experience something of this in the art forms created by those in whose lives one is already sharing, and of course the great artist whom one has never met or from a previous age was also human and spoke from his inner life to ours.

These reflections can be applied to the use of the projected picture before a large gathering, with perhaps a musical commentary, or accompanied by poetry, or with a brief bidding prayer. There is also great scope for displays of pupils' art, both graphic and plastic, accompanied by the reading of pupils' poetry. This is often particularly effective in smaller groups.

Meditation is usually not assisted by controversy, and particularly in the county school controversy is a vital aspect of assembly. It would be better to think of county school assemblies as being divided into the meditative type and the controversial type rather than trying to mix them.

Literature may be useful in worship when it offers through the identification of the hearer with its content (and more rarely its form) a vehicle for self-transformation.[6] But the transformation offered by the literature must be compatible with the ideals and objectives of religion. These will include self-transcendence, self-criticism and the awakening of the insights and attitudes described by certain existentialists as 'authentic existence'. There are of course various kinds of formation effected through literature which are not acceptable to religion. Pornography, for example, deforms the human.

In the voluntary Christian worship offered by the church school the Bible can be read as the word of God. This is not appropriate in the assembly of the county school. The relationship between the creator and the creature which is affirmed in the expression 'the word of God' is absolute. It is typically religious. The word of God makes a royal demand, a proclamation of divine judgment and mercy. Not only does this absoluteness itself prohibit the use of the Bible as the

word of God in the county assembly but there are various
claimants to the title 'word of God'. The educational
establishment as such is not competent to decide which if
any shall indeed be heard as God's word.

But the county school is not competent to deny a claim
to be the word of God either. The Bible, therefore, must not
be read as merely literature but as being at least literature. It
will be read, like other literature, because of its power to
offer transformation through the identification of the
hearers, but it is also the literature of the church where it not
only presents the images transformed (art) but the reality
blended with the image (salvation history).

Experiential methods of teaching the Bible are based on
the belief that the experience of modern Western man is
continuous with that of ancient Semitic man. Every modern
experience is said to have its ancient counterpart. Although
this approach presents difficulties, it is the best available to
the assembly in any school. The reason for this is that
whatever its hermeneutical problems, the experiential
approach may at least be valid educationally. This is true of
only one other way of treating the Bible: the approach
through the phenomenology of religion in which the Bible is
seen as the religious literature of the Judeao-Christian
tradition and is to be studied alongside other religious
literature. But unless it contains an existential dimension, the
phenomenological approach to the Bible cannot be related to
any of the facets of worship described in chapter 2. Although
educationally valid, it is less suitable as part of a theory of
worship, pre-worship or assembly in the school. This leaves the
experiential approach as the most suitable one for assembly.
When studied through the experiential method, the Bible offers
a realignment of the self image; the phenomenological method
may have this effect but this is not its prime purpose. The
phenomenological approach is most at home in the classroom
where religion is studied.

Exactly the same considerations apply to the use of the
Koran in assembly in the county school. It cannot be read as
the word of God. It must be presented as being at least
literature, since there is a community which hails it as the
divine word. It must be treated as being personally illumi-
nating and not simply as the religious literature of Islam. As

far as the problem of the experiential continuity is concerned, the gulf between the man of seventh-century Arabia and modern man is no greater than that between the Hebrew man and today.

6   *The School Assembly*

The school assembly has considerable educational potential. When it is taken up with worship, something is being done which in the county school ought not to be attempted at all in that form, and in the meantime, the opportunity to do something more directly related to the tasks of the school is missed. Corporate, compulsory worship should be abandoned, and assembly then left free to relate in new ways to the curriculum. The positive gains of such assemblies will be discussed as we continue.

The objectives of school assembly will be to provide ceremonies, celebrations and other events which, while not assuming the truth of any one controversial statement, will present the issues to the pupils in a way so as

1. To widen the pupil's repertoire of appropriate emotional response. An appropriate emotional response is one which in terms of the surrounding society is proportioned to the circumstances which evoke it. A person who flies into a fury if he loses his fountain pen but is unmoved by the human need in the great city around him has inappropriate emotions. A person who is not moved by the beautiful and who never feels compassion is lacking in emotional breadth. It is, of course, impossible to avoid some degree of cultural definition of what an appropriate emotional response is, but the assembly would attempt to introduce the emotions and responses of other cultures. The controlling criterion in the education of the emotions will be the ethical status of the emotion in relation to its stimulus. At no point can education evade the responsibility of making this sort of ethical judgment.

2. To encourage a reflective approach to living, a way

which transcends the immediacy of experience. Man's capacity for reflection upon himself and his worth is part of his distinctive existence. Heidegger has pointed out that to *ek-sist* is to stand out, to project above. Man is self-aware being. To live immersed in one's world instead of being in critical action and reaction with one's world is to lose part of being human.

3. To demonstrate the values which are not controversial and upon which democratic society depends. These values include freedom of speech, respect for the rights of minorities, the equality before the law and in education of all religious and ethnic groups, and responsibility for personal decision-making and for participation in community decision-making.[1]

4. To provide some experience and understanding of what worship is so that the way of worship, along with other life styles, will remain an option for anyone who wishes to follow it and so that all will have some insight into what it is like to live a religious life. But this provision will not require any one to worship and will certainly not commit the school to corporate acts of worship.

These objectives are chosen because they are consistent with many of the functions which the assembly already has. Assembly is of course often valued by schools for reasons other than religious ones. The objectives, particularly the second and the fourth ones, offer some continuity with present school worship. The first three objectives relate to central concerns of education and the last one is a contribution from religious education. The objectives are not exhaustive. Other subjects of the curriculum will be able to add other objectives.

In relation to the tradition of worship, the tasks of these assemblies will be to select from the various aspects of worship those which

(*a*) are low in cognitive content and which therefore do not commit the pupil and the staff member to beliefs which they may not have, or

(*b*) are high in cognitive content but which can be treated in a controversial and not an affirmative manner, and finally

(*c*) are compatible with educational goals, e.g. can be treated in an open way, and contribute to the moral, aesthetic and religious development of the pupil in a rational, freedom-enhancing way.

Should such assemblies be compulsory? At the moment compulsory school worship is the most objectionable example of compulsion which the school offers its pupils. It will hardly do to claim that pupils are also compelled to study various subjects and to sit examinations and so on. Not only is it most unwise in view of the growing opinion which rejects compulsion within education in any form for religious education to shelter within such a claim, but there is in any case a difference between compelling a boy to play sport when he does not enjoy sport or compelling him to take three subjects when he would rather only take two, and compelling him to worship God when he does not believe in God. The latter may be a direct infringement of his conscience. It involves him not only in constraint but in hypocrisy. Religious education has been the peak of the compulsion offered by our school system and worship has been the most objectionable aspect of compulsory religion. Such compulsion could never have been carried through at all without the escape clause, which is rightly called the 'conscience clause' and has acted as a safety valve.

But if the following conditions are met, then the aspects of compulsion which are particularly objectionable in the case of school worship will disappear. The question of compulsion in assembly will then be on the same footing as questions of compulsion in other parts of school life. This may not be a great asset but at least it removes a disadvantage and brings assembly up to the starting line.

The conditions are

(*a*) the conscience of staff and pupils must not be compromised;

(*b*) a false impression must not be given of the status of religious belief or the role of religious life;

(*c*) motivation must be provided by educational rather than by evangelistic or indoctrinatory goals.

There is no reason why the sort of assemblies being described here should take place every day. Daily worship is a relic of monastic discipline, of a daily devotional order which presupposed a certain type of spirituality. Nor need such assemblies take the form of the whole school gathered together. Small gatherings of a dozen or so may sometimes not only be more effective in themselves but may avoid the association of God with the school hierarchy. Instead of thinking of school assembly as worship and the classes as education, we should simply look at the various groupings which may be formed for various purposes in a school. Open plan schools lend themselves easily to this conception. Already teachers in such schools are accustomed to ask what may best be done with several pupils, what may best be done with thirty, and what best with three hundred. Large assemblies should simply be included in this pattern of planning, as being in no way distinct, except that they will contain those things most suitable for large gatherings and, in the light of the criteria outlined, they will seek to draw out the inner relationship between education, democracy and the nature of man. We would then envisage some means in each school whereby the various kinds of vertical or horizontal groups (sixth form only, or house or family groups) plus occasional smaller, more intimate groups, might meet at various times for meditation, celebration and other activities which would express the values in mind.

Perhaps in many secondary schools, the best way to arrange such assemblies would be through an Assembly Committee, which would consist of various members of staff and pupils, chosen from various subject areas and representing various religious and non-religious viewpoints. The chairman of the committee would be a teacher aware of the humane depths of the curriculum. He might be the religious education specialist, but this need not be the case, and if a suitable teacher can be found who works in some other subject area, it might guard against any misunderstanding. Some teachers of religion are people with an understanding of the implications of education as a whole for the life of man and others are not. The same is true of teachers of other subjects. The committee would meet for a whole day early in the term to plan the large assemblies for the following term. Ideally they would have in front of them the various syllabuses and other proposals for the subject work in the following term, so that, with help from the various heads of departments, connections would be spotted and common themes drawn out. Assembly would thus be not an irrelevant interlude before the educational work of the school begins, but the centre for the illumination and integration of the whole curriculum.

There would then be no more intimate connection between religious education and the assembly than there would be between any other subject and the assembly. Religious education must disown the present form of school worship and must be ready to set the assembly free to serve the whole curriculum.[2]

What educational potential would such assemblies have? The relation between the school and the community has been growing more intimate in recent years, but one still finds a few schools where apart from sporadic prayers for 'the nations of the world' and 'the leaders of industry' the potential of the school assembly for extroverting the school is not explored. Assembly is the appropriate place for studies through music, drama, poetry and slides of urban problems, of local government and of the environment. Sometimes assembly for a whole week can be devoted to a particular country, with displays of work from the geography department, recorded music and visiting speakers. Pupils with pen friends abroad may read the letters they have received from them, and schools with a connection with a school abroad may centre some programmes around the life of the sister school, with the playing of message tapes. If religion is an issue in the country being dealt with, this would be treated as one way of understanding the hopes and ideals of the country. The missionary societies (as they are still sometimes called) of the various churches provide in their audio-visual aid catalogues a good range of materials which can be used to document such assemblies. This kind of assembly will not be a geography lesson or a religious education class, although it may have links with both. The emphasis is not upon the technical aspects of subject disciplines, but upon the humanitarian aspects. In studying China in assembly, one does not study the mechanics and movements and quantities of the Chinese iron and steel industry but one reads from the writings of Confucius, Mao Tse Tung, and the Chinese poets and philosophers. One considers some of the problems relating to China's role in the world today and one might include a programme on education in China. The aims are to create some understanding of the aspirations of the Chinese people, their contributions to the life of man today in the broadest religious, artistic, social and political manner. These are the sorts of things which can often be done quite briefly with only a few words and a picture, but which if supported by more detailed and technical study in smaller groups, can be enriching and can add considerably to the sense of the unity of several areas of study.

There is another difference between an assembly of this sort and the classroom lesson. The pupil is engaged at another level of his self-understanding. In assembly he sees himself as a member of the school, or at least of the upper school, or whatever, and not simply as a member of the form or the English set or the second eleven under-thirteens. He sees members of the school taking part, fellow pupils from other subject areas and other age groups, he sees members of staff normally met only in the laboratory or the library or at the staff room door. The school assembly is the mass medium of the school and it can have all the influence and prestige which the mass media have in society at large. This influence must be carefully cultivated so as to become a force in the curriculum.

Not only can the assembly become a sort of window on the world, turning the school towards the life of man as a whole, but it can also be used to heighten awareness of current affairs not only with a view to deepening concern for others but in order to strengthen the pupil's own sense of participation in the community and to help him to form attitudes about moral, social, religious and political matters through hearing some of the relevant facts and arguments. To the question: Why cannot this be done in class?, the answer is that it often can be done in class quite well and some aspects can only be done in class, but there will be times when a wider forum will give a sense of dignity, of significance, and of total school involvement. Weeks of programmes should thus be devoted to issues such as the personal and national use of money, the use of work and leisure, problems created by advances in medicine and the question of human rights. Methods of presentation might include panels of teachers and pupils commenting or giving a prepared answer to a question, displays of posters with perhaps some description by the

designers, readings from newspapers and the playing of taped
and recorded items from radio and television broadcasts and
the reading of letters and essays written by both staff and
pupils, with replies.

Weeks like this would often be linked with practical
concerns. The group who put up the tents for the Darby and
Joan Club fair would report on the event, and so on.

In assemblies of this sort the nettle of controversy must be
grasped very firmly. The fear of debate which emaciates
many a school assembly must be overcome if any progress is
to be made in turning the assembly into an educational
contribution to the curriculum. Calm, clear and informed
controversy is the very life blood of the moral, social and
religious education of young people today. It is not harmful
to young people to realize that members of staff are not
unanimous about important matters of public concern. The
silent school or the one inhibited by an imposed unanimity
or by the use of a headmaster's veto (decisions about content
should be the responsibility of the Assembly Committee) will
be a poor place for members of the free and pluralistic
society to test their criteria.

This is particularly true when we consider the use of the
assembly in the teaching of democracy. The practice of
holding mock elections during times of national election
should be more widespread, especially now that eighteen-
year-olds have the vote, and assembly would be the right
place for this to take place. Speeches from student candidates
and from the actual party candidates should find a place in
assembly.

The main current concern of the life of the school should
be displayed in the assembly. The clubs and societies should
hold an annual fair, taking lunchtimes and assemblies to
present their activities to the rest of the school. The careers
staff or the counselling services should also have a week.

This leads us to think of some of the ways in which the
assembly might help to relate the various topics covered in
class by the different subject departments. This is already
taking place in the junior school, although a large number of
head teachers do not believe that the school assembly in the
junior school should be related to the curriculum.[3] The
problem is more significant in the secondary school. Sixth

forms working on an integrated general studies course will find plenty of ideas, but in other forms the severity of the fragmentation of knowledge may be seen from the fact that it is often difficult to find any way in which the subjects share a common interest or contribute in any way to the resolution of a common problem. Weeks of assemblies exploring a theme on 'what the subjects say' may be of help. Biology, history, religious studies, music, literature, physics and others may join a symposium on what the subjects have to say about war, about the future of man, about cities, about the imagination, about love, fear and death. This could be done through interviews of 'A' level students by those from other subjects, comments by subject teachers, and reports from groups of pupils who have been working on their subject's contribution to the topic. Often the weeks devoted to social and international affairs will also show how the subjects are one.[4]

Finally in this short list of suggestions, it may be noted that assemblies of this sort possess the added advantage of throwing members of staff together in the discussions and planning which must precede them. Subject barriers exist in the classroom because they exist in the staff room. Some teachers may be encouraged in this way to explore the human implications of their own subject more deeply, and this in turn will affect the quality of their teaching.[5]

Each subject will have its contribution to assembly, and people of various faiths will interpret assembly in various ways. This ambiguity is deliberately present in the assemblies suggested. It is possible for Christians and those interested in religious education to understand these assemblies as being a threshold for worship, i.e. as containing aspects of worship and as being a preparation for an appreciation of what worship involves. This interpretation is not required by the sort of assemblies we have described but it is a possible one.

We have seen that worship is an expression of ultimate concern. This is seen clearly in the hymn by F.W. Faber (1814-63):

> My God, how wonderful thou art,
>   Thy majesty how bright,
> How beautiful they mercy-seat
>   In depths of burning light!

> How dread are thine eternal years,
>   O everlasting Lord,
> By prostrate spirits night and day
>   Incessantly adored!
>
> How beautiful, how beautiful
>   The sight of thee must be,
> Thine endless wisdom, boundless power,
>   And awful purity!

This profoundly worshipful hymn gains its effect because it not only expresses beliefs about God but responds to those beliefs. The famous lines of W. Chalmers Smith (1824-1908) form an interesting contrast:

> Immortal, invisible, God only wise,
> In light inaccessible hid from our eyes,
> Most blessed, most glorious, the Ancient of Days,
> Almighty, victorious, they great name we praise.
>
> Unresting, unhasting, and silent as light,
> Nor wanting, nor wasting, thou rulest in might;
> Thy justice like mountains high soaring above
> Thy clouds which are fountains of goodness and love.

The first person is largely lacking in Smith's hymn. God is described in measured theological language. But in Faber's hymn, the emotions of the believer are important. Lines in the later verses such as 'O how I fear Thee, living God' and 'Yet I may love thee too, O Lord', the reference to the tears of the believer and his deep feelings as he worships, the use of words such as 'beautiful' (three times), 'wonderful', 'dread' and 'awful' conjure up the atmosphere of numinous presence by listing those aspects of the divine about which the worshipper feels most deeply. But in Smith's lines, although there is certainly a cumulative effect which rises to a climax in the last verse, the epithets used of God are in the main abstract and objective. Faber's hymn is more worshipful because it is more emotional, but that is not all. It is emotional in that it reminds the worshipper how deeply the being of God concerns him, that it is God and no one else who is the object of his fear, his dread, his love. The emotion in the hymn reaches such intensity because it gathers around what the hymn unfolds as the believer's object of deepest concern.

The words, however, fail to express anything of final concern, or of concern at all, to many of the pupils in school assembly who sing them. Shall we make them read the words carefully first? Will the head teacher give a short explanation of the hymn? But even if their understanding deepens, will their concern increase?

Christian nurture in the church has developed what can be called a ladder of concern intended to lead people through the things in their daily lives about which they are most deeply concerned until they reach the level of ultimate concern for God. So the return of the sun after the winter solstice was celebrated and linked to the entry into the world of Christ the true light. The gathering of the harvest was an occasion for teaching about God as Creator and so for helping people to see beyond their daily concern for bread to the Lord of all life. The way the ceremonies of the church clustered around the great crises of life, birth, marriage and death is another example of teaching people to see the deeper meaning of what already mattered deeply to them.

All the symbolism of the church may be thought of in this way. When the worshipper partakes in the Eucharist he does so surrounded by symbols; the burning candles, the white cloth, the wooden cross, the bread and the wine, all are elements taken from the daily lives of the worshippers and made the vehicle of deeper significance. These objects are called 'aids to worship', and they assist worship because they extend the concern of the worshipper for light and food until it becomes concern for the light of the world and the bread of life. The worshipper is invited to meditate on something about which he has a genuine and legitimate but limited concern until he perceives beyond it that about which, as he comes through worship to realize again and again, his concern is unlimited.

Many school assemblies are fiercely Protestant in that there is no symbolism except words and bodily postures. Pupils are encouraged to meditate directly upon God without passing through a ladder of concern. In other schools there is an attempt to introduce symbolism. Religious pictures hang

on the walls, a lectern carved with doves or flames stands at
the front, or there may even be a cross on the table. Such
efforts rarely have the desired result. This is because symbols
only have power if two conditions are fulfilled. The symbols
must share in the character of that to which they point and
they must spring out of the genuine concerns of the
worshipper. Such religious symbols do not fulfill this second
condition, and because they are incapable of pointing beyond
themselves, they become pious and formal irrelevancies.

Instead of starting from the religious end and trying to
make the rungs of the ladder reach further down, we must
start from the other end and ask what our pupils are
genuinely concerned about. They may be concerned about
their families and friends, about their own health and their
hobbies, about their success and failure at games and studies,
and about their futures. Many of the older students will be
developing a concern for the society in which they live and
its problems of labour and loneliness, conditions and developments in their own towns. Some, too, will be growing into an
awareness of the world-wide community and will work
eagerly and unselfishly for charities such as Oxfam, and some
will debate with a high degree of involvement the rights and
wrongs of international situations.

What we shall try to do then in assembly is to encourage
the members of the school to consider seriously their most
pressing concerns, in the hope that they will be led from the
trivial to the significant, from that which is of immediate
concern to that which is of lasting concern, to the things
which are the finally serious concerns of life. Specific
contents can only be offered in specific school situations.
Nevertheless, pupils who engage in this sort of assembly will
be experiencing a small aspect of what Christians do when
they worship; assembly will have become a threshold of
worship for them.

In the hymn 'My God, how wonderful thou art' the first
three verses consist of affirmation, the last three of response.
God is affirmed as wonderful, beautiful, majestic, wise and
pure. Each affirmation concludes with an exclamation mark,
emphasizing the bold and startling nature of what is being
said. This recital or re-emphasis of the qualities of the object
of concern is a feature of most worship.

For young children this is the most natural aspect of any preparation for worship. The experiences of delight, wonder and joy in life and movement, in growing things and in the development of skills, these are for the young child the roots of any later experience of worship. At the secondary level, the young person's deepened knowledge of himself and his world will probably mean that worship as concern will be more meaningful than worship as affirmation. But there will still be a place in school assembly for the expression of delight in movement and music, in art and literature, and to affirm the joy of creativity in various ways.

In worship the prayer of adoration and thanksgiving finds some of its characteristic intentions in expressions of concern and affirmation. What of petition and intercession?

> O Lord Jesus Christ, our Maker and Redeemer, who by thy providence hast made us what we are: thou hast a purpose for us; do thou, O Lord, in thy mercy, fulfill in us thy purpose. Thou alone art wisdom; thou knowest what may benefit sinners such as we are; do thou, in thy mercy, direct our future, according to thy will, as seemest best in the eyes of thy majesty, O Jesus Christ, our Lord.[6]

What does the petitioner hope that this prayer will accomplish? One might get the impression that he hopes to be relieved of the responsibility for deciding his own future, since phrases such as 'Thou alone art wisdom' and 'direct our future' suggest that supernatural intervention is expected. Most Christians would today regard such an expectation as an abuse of prayer. The prayer is surely intended to be not a disavowal but an acceptance of responsibility and an aspiration towards more responsible decision. It will be more responsible because the factors mentioned in the prayer, God's mercy, his purpose, the divine will, have been set again before the believer's mind by his prayer. Let us take another example.

> O God, by whom the humble are guided in judgment, and light riseth up in darkness for the faithful, grant to us in all our doubts and perplexities the grace to ask what thou wouldst have us do, that the spirit of wisdom may save us from false choices, and that in thy light we may see light,

and in thy straight path may not stumble; through our Saviour Jesus Christ.[7]

It is clear in this prayer that the actual decision is to be made by the petitioner. He sees the possibility of making the wrong choice. The purpose of his prayer is that he may 'see light in thy light'. So he lays his life before God in meditation, thinking about the choices which face him and hoping that his insight will be clarified as he prays. The prayer reminds him that his decision must be made in a humble spirit and that it must be in harmony with the highest known to him, all the name 'Jesus Christ' signifies.

From these examples we can see that an important part of what happens in prayer is that the believer seeks to place some particular action within the context of his general orientation in life. He believes that his decision will be made more wisely if it is made in the light of his deepest values and long range aims.

There are a number of difficulties about praying in assembly. One difficulty is that prayer is increasingly an alien activity to young people. Of course, no prayer can be used in the county school assembly if it purports to be spoken on behalf of everyone present. The whole of our previous discussion would rule out the possibility of the county school being asked or required to say the Lord's Prayer together. That is an activity suitable only for a Christian community. But there is no reason why religion should not be mentioned in assembly from time to time. It is wholly appropriate that when a priest or layman has been leading a series of assemblies, he should conclude with the words: 'I am going to pray a prayer much loved by my fellow believers. I hope you will enjoy·listening to it.' Since it does not commit the listeners and does not purport to represent anything other than the views of the speaker and his co-religionists, such a procedure seems quite unobjectionable. Indeed, it is often found that such prayers are listened to with rather more interest and respect than is usually the case in school assembly.

But even with the completely secular assemblies we have discussed, it is open to the believer in prayer to interpret their relevance to prayer in the following way. As with other aspects of worship, we must select something from prayer, one of the attitudes involved in praying and one which may stand a chance of being understood and actually experienced. This element will be used to develop a fuller understanding of what prayer means. The reorientation of one's life in the light of one's deepest values is one such element, and its relation to prayer can perhaps be shown in the religious education classroom.

As an illustration, let us suppose that assemblies for a week will be on the theme 'Vocation'. There will be no hymns, prayers or readings from the Bible. On the Monday an educational psychologist attached to the authority will give a short talk about the factors which form a decision about employment. Pupils will be invited to write 'letters to the editor' expressing their reactions to this and the following talks. On Tuesday the careers counsellor will be interviewed by one of the older students. 'Our work is largely fixed for us by the subjects we choose for "O" levels or even earlier before the implications are clear to us. Is this fair and what can be done about it?' 'What can be said in favour of the idea that the schools should be directed by the government to produce so many teachers, so many engineers and so on and when the quota is full you have to select your next choice?' On Wednesday a local clergyman, perhaps one who entered the priesthood later in life, will talk about 'God and your job'. This is included because religion is often an important factor in the work decision of many people, perhaps especially those notable for service to others. Obviously no exclusive claims for religion can be made in this connection and one day in five is probably about the right proportion. It should certainly not be the final day of the series, in case the impression should be given that everything else was leading up to this. Such an ending of the series would tend to rob the earlier days of their own integrity, reducing them to the status of preparation for the important day. On Thursday a panel of pupils can read excerpts from pupils' letters and on Friday the headmaster could comment on some of the letters or offer some reflections about the week.

If during some such week as this, even a few young people are encouraged to think about the general direction which their lives are taking, if they realize more of the factors involved, if they are challenged to ask themselves if what they are deciding is guided by the best they know, have they not been doing at least part of what the religious man does when he prays that 'the spirit of true wisdom may save us from all false choices'? This is certainly one way to introduce the idea and practice of meditation, especially if at some points music followed by a short silence is used, and it may provide some indirect introduction to the understanding of petitionary prayer.

Intercessary prayer arises out of an outgoing love for others. You may love others without praying for them but you may not truly pray for them unless you love them. The pharisee did not pray for the sinner who stood beside him because there was no compassion in his heart, but behind the prayer 'Father forgive them' lay a whole life devoted to loving service. Prayer cannot be simply defined as the love of others but it does spring from this love. The spirit of prayer includes the spirit of unselfish love although that does not exhaust the meaning of prayer. Love is one of the essential elements of intercession and it is because of this and the fact that it is the aspect of prayer which everybody can experience that it can offer another threshold for the spiritual life. The school will not understand prayer until it understands love. It may not understand prayer even when it understands love but at least a start will have been made.

Let us suppose that the theme for the week is 'Children' and that the object is to encourage a concern for the needs of children. This theme could be developed through a series of Bible readings including some about Jesus and children, hymns about children and prayers for children of many lands. But such a programme would have failed to set the prayers in a real context of human caring. The children in the gospel stories are described in the briefest of terms; few of the real interests and problems of childhood are to be found in them. The purpose of the evangelists was not to tell us about children but to tell us something about Jesus and his teaching. For those who saw his behaviour towards children it no doubt appeared loving, although this is not referred to very much, and as such it would have flowed back into their own friendships and into their communion with God. But for the children and young people listening today in assembly, it is just another reading from the Bible. The living spirit of prayer must be sought again and again in the present moment of compassion. It can never be captured and conveyed by books. The stories in the books only become significant to pupils after they have met children, loved them, served them and perhaps suffered with them and such experience is essential in order to provide a pre-understanding of the gospel stories and of the spirit of prayer.

Let us try a different approach. On Monday we will have a social worker come and tell us about the children she meets in her daily work. On Tuesday an inspector from the National Society for the Prevention of Cruelty to Children will visit and be interviewed and on Wednesday there will be someone from Dr Barnardo's homes. On Thursday a talk can be given about the Save the Children Fund. These talks will be set into a programme which will contain other activities and reports and the whole series will be the hub of special activities on the theme at other times of the day. If the week is timed so as to coincide with a national children's appeal then a competition (no prizes!) could be held for the best poster publicizing the week which could be displayed in nearby shops, churches and schools. Money can be raised and toys collected. The humanities department might be able to stage an exhibition dealing with children in many lands. In assembly, after each talk, a group of pupils might be able to sing a children's song from abroad. One form might be given the task of maintaining a display board during the week of newspaper cuttings dealing with children's exploits and dangers. A programme of films about children's welfare can be shown one lunch time. The sixth form might be able to get up a concert party and pay a visit one evening to a children's home or take some children to the zoo. If it is desired to include some prayers, and if these can be offered as the contribution of one individual and not as the belief of all, this can usefully be done on the Friday. The prayer will not be just part of the daily routine, but will already have been present in the other actions, words, music and pictures of the week. But even if prayer is not actually offered, the basis of caring out of which this particular spirituality springs will have been widened. Needy children are not for the sake of prayer, but prayer and love are for needy children.

These then must serve as examples of the way that religious education may interpret the school assembly. It must be emphasized again that other subjects may find other ways in which their own humanitarian intentions may be focussed in the assembly. The only respect in which religion has any special claim upon assembly is the sense in which both worship and education are related, in Christian thought, to the image of God in man, the one concerned to adore him in whose likeness man is made, the other to help restore that fragmented and distorted glory.

It has already been remarked that in assemblies of this kind there is no need at all to exclude religion any more than any subject should be excluded, and there are some grounds for thinking that religion may have a particularly important role to play, different though it will be from its traditional role. Prayer, for example, can be used in assembly provided people are given clearly to understand that they are not expected to identify with the prayer and that it does not purport to express their own faith. They must be allowed to bow their heads or to merely listen as they see fit.

Hymn singing presents special difficulties because unlike praying it is necessarily a corporate activity. It depends on how seriously the words of hymns are to be taken. It would be tactless and pedantic if a Christian argued that a humanist was inconsistent in singing the National Anthem because it is a prayer addressed to God. The National Anthem is a symbol of national unity. The theological significance of the words is not prominent in the function of the anthem as it is actually used and that is as it should be. Some people might take that general attitude towards some of the well-established traditional hymns sung in assemblies. It is possible indeed that school assembly has in the minds of a good many parents, city councillors and politicians very much the same sort of general moral and national significance which the singing of the National Anthem has. So it seems pedantic to go carefully through these hymns picking out verses and odd expressions which imply Christian belief.

On the other hand, our whole discussion implies that assembly should be taken fairly seriously. It seems best then not to use in assembly hymns which emphasize personal commitment or inner devotional awareness. Hymns like

'Take my life' and 'O Jesus I have promised' are unsuitable for school assembly. At the same time, more attention should be given to the rapidly growing number of songs expressing various humane and religious values but not committing the singers to unanimity in Christian belief.[8]

But once it is accepted that school assembly is a time of sharing of ideals and visions rather than of requiring from all a unanimous worship, the range of subjects and attitudes which can be expressed there is wide. There is, for example, no reason at all why the Christian Union should not be encouraged to take a week to present their case. Let them say what they believe and why; let them sing their songs and share their prayers. And next week, let any atheists or secular humanists who may be in the school community explain their views as well.

Are there any limits to this tolerance? From its nature as open, free, critical, rational, ethical and person-centred, education must draw the strength to gaze even at the things which, if it were to succumb to them, would destroy it. There seems no reason why in secondary schools statements from extreme right wing and left wing points of view should not be heard provided they are presented in a manner compatible with the educational ideals.

Totalitarianism of all sorts would destroy the possibility of the education described here, but to refuse a platform to such points of view would be for education to cease to enquire and thus to destroy itself before it was destroyed. This is surely the right response to those who urge that Christians must indoctrinate, i.e. maintain the totalitarian grip of unquestioning obedience and insistent repetition of assumed religious truth, because if Christians do not, advocates of less desirable points of view will be less delicate. Such views strike at the fundamental connection between Christian faith and education. They posit a view of Christian faith with which only instruction is compatible. It is true that the sort of educational ideal described here is the enemy of that sort of Christian faith. But education is the friend and partner of that Christian faith which is chosen deliberately in the presence of known and understood alternatives, and which, when chosen, continues to claim for others that same freedom to choose, and continues in hopeful dialogue with the alternatives it has rejected.

There is another possible objection to the type of assembly described here. Based as it is specifically on a view of man, and holding that education is what it is because of that view, is there not a danger of an indoctrination into that view, an indoctrination all the more subtle because it avoids explicit enforcement of dogmas? But if one has a view of man which sees him as attaining rational and ethical autonomy, such a view cannot be compatible with indoctrination, which would deprive people of their autonomy, which deliberately seeks to bypass the reason, and which is for those reasons itself an unethical process. Moreover, this view of man would itself be challenged. Other views of the person involving different conceptions of freedom, for example, may receive a hearing. This is what is meant by claiming that education must have the courage to include even the things which have the potential for nullifying education. The educational process so understood and the assembly which focuses it contains inbuilt guarantees against becoming indoctrinatory.

Such assemblies will not seek to secure commitment, nor to profess faith but to deepen understanding and to facilitate choice. Religious education has nothing to lose from such a development and much to gain. For the assembly itself, the options are clear. It either moves into the centre of the curriculum and of the educational ideal or it remains on the sidelines, increasingly isolated from the work of the religious education department and ignored by everyone else except those few in whose interest it is that an attempt should be made to use religion to make young people orderly and docile.

Appendix

A Comparison of the Cambridgeshire Syllabuses of 1924 and 1939

1924
Religion and Corporate Life in the School

1939
Religion and Corporate Life in the School

'The Wind of the Spirit bloweth as it listeth, and we know not whence it cometh or whither it goeth, and so is everyone who is born of the Spirit.'[1] We cannot narrow religious teaching down to the limits of a syllabus, no matter how wide that syllabus may be. All Education rightly conceived is religious education, and it may happen that many a pupil will gain a deeper knowledge of God and of His dealings with men from History, Literature, Science or other lessons than from the Bible lesson. We may, in any case, be certain that unless all the teaching throughout the school is infused with a sense of earnest enquiry[3] and with a conviction of the reality of God's presence among men, the specific Religious Instruction, like all isolated and detached knowledge, will be sterile and uninspiring.

The Bible to be understood must be translated into terms of our own experience,[4] and although this is a life-long task to which there is no short cut in the school room, yet children may see that not only Samuel, but also Joan of Arc, heard the voice of God and was obedient to the call;

All education rightly conceived is religious education.[2]

Specific religious instruction, like any isolated and detailed knowledge, will be sterile and uninspiring unless all the teaching throughout the school is infused with the appreciation of goodness, beauty and truth,[3] with the conviction of the reality of God's presence among men, and embraces conduct no less than learning.

that Abraham Lincoln, like Isaiah, had a statesman's message to his country; and that Linnaeus, no less than Moses, worshipped the vision of God revealed in burning bush.

But the child learns primarily by doing. How he lives is of more importance for his development than what he studies.[5] Thus the critical question in Religious Education must be, so far as the school is concerned, Is the School a Christian Community? Does membership in the School give a training in Christian character?

So far, therefore, as the school is concerned, the critical question in religious education must be: Is the school a Christian community? Does membership in the school give a training in Christian character?

The religious atmosphere of the school and the religious development of the child in it depend first and foremost on the teacher's personality and the ideals and faith behind it. The spiritual, as has often been pointed out, is more commonly caught than taught. The personal reverence, both outward and inward, of the teacher is of immeasurable importance. The wakening and guidance of the spiritual sense in the children is the first factor in creating the finest fruit in individual character and, consequently, in the happiness and right development of the race. The responsibility of the teacher towards the spiritual growth of the child is no whit less than towards the intellectual and physical, not only because some children receive little help in this respect at home, but also because education is one and indivisible; if the child is to be taught well, body, mind and spirit must be taught together.

Since children learn by what they themselves do even more

We must first clear our minds by studying the Beatitudes, and the standard of values revealed to us in the Parables. We can then ask ourselves pertinent questions as to our methods of organisation and discipline, and as to the value set in the school on the various interests that move children and the actions that result. Does the school routine encourage emulation and competition?[7] or is it organised so as to make co-operation easy? Are there opportunities for the stronger to help the weaker? Is a love of animals inculcated? Not only games but also work can be organised so that the child's natural desire to excel is robbed of its selfishness by his keenness to help his 'side', his 'group', his 'House' or his 'team', and every member of it.[8] Has each individual child as far as possible an opportunity to use his talent, however small? The glory of losing self cannot be realised if the self has never been discovered. If we have a prefect system, do our leaders naturally act as the 'servants of all', or are they little tyrants in the making?[9]

Has the whole school, as well as each individual, plenty of opportunities for realising the joy of service?

What does the school do for the village or town? –for the parents? — what does the Infants' Department do for the Senior Department?

What do the children do for the school? The isolated, unhelpful, unproductive life, however blameless, is not the Christian life.

than by what another teaches them in class, the whole ordering of the school can and should contribute to religious instruction in the wider sense. It should guide with sympathy the various interests both in work and play which move children and govern their actions. Such questions as the following, based on the standards revealed in Beatitude and Parable, should be constantly before the Headmaster or Headmistress:[6]

Is the school so organised as to encourage co-operation as well as proper forms of competition?[7] Are opportunities given whereby the stronger and cleverer[8] may help the weaker?

Is love of animals, birds, flowers, etc., inculcated?

What does the child do for his school?

What does the school do for the village or town, or for wider causes, such as homeless children, hospitals or missions overseas?[10]

'I am come that ye may have life and have it more abundantly.' It is extremely important that as life opens before them boys and girls should realise that 'life abounding' is a mark of God's inspiration.[11] The school, too, must emphasise 'Thou shalt' — and not 'Thou shalt not'. Without self-control and self-denial nothing of value can be accomplished, and a child soon learns this lesson, but it is of no value to him to learn to abstain from doing or speaking for the mere sake of abstaining. He must be able every year he grows to see more and more the reason for his abstinence and for his self-control. When every child thinks first of the common good and controls himself with that end in view, perfect discipline is reached. For true discipline is not an order imposed from without, and forced on the pupils, but is formed naturally from within and accepted by them. The free child is one who is learning daily to control and to direct himself.[12]

Does it take pains to enrich home-life by inspiring the child?

Is the grace of courtesy (one aspect of Christian love) taught and encouraged?[11] Is the school emphasising 'Thou shalt' as the rule of conduct, rather than 'Thou shalt not'?

Is the child learning 'self-reverance, self-knowledge, self-control', as well as school lessons?

On the practical answer to such questions as these depend to an important extent the Christian atmosphere of the school and the development of Christian character in it.

The learning of two great lessons forms the basis of all the detailed instruction. The first and great commandment has not ceased to be, Thou shalt love the Lord thy God with all thy mind and with all thy strength. Without faith in the Holiest, the impulse to goodness cannot but weaken and its standards decline. Without faith in the Father, the brotherhood of man is left without foundation. The second and consequent lesson, the love of our neighbour, with the obligation towards others that it entails, is the charter of the common good, and involves for every child those issues of self-control and self-denial which build up the happy society. The best of all discipline is self-discipline, and it is learned naturally under the Christian inspiration.[12] The religious and spiritual side of education has thus a function of immeasurable importance both in the formation of individual character and also in the creation of a finer citizenship and a better world.

In all this work the teacher has the example of Jesus Christ, who

In this his highest task the teacher has the example of Jesus himself adopted the life of a Teacher,[13] gave full play to the individuality of His disciples, and relied on no system of external organisation in His dealings with them.

Christ who gave full play of the individuality of His disciples, and relied on no system of external organisation in His dealings with them. And he can pass to his pupils no greater or more lasting gift than to quicken their admiration of that unique personality, and to fill them with the desire to know Him better, to be like Him, and to work in His service.[13]

Corporate Prayer[14]
The centre and focus of such a corporate ideal will naturally be the time when the school comes together for prayer. Morning Assembly should be welcomed as the opportunity for the dedication of all the school life and work. 'It should not be merely an opening ceremony, but a preparation for the day, the influence of which will be felt throughout the day.'

Morning Assembly will be welcomed as the opportunity for the dedication of all the school life and work.

The teacher must strive by the reverence of his own demeanour, as in the presence of God, to create the sense of worship and enable the children to feel that he is really praying the prayers which he speaks. Accordingly it is of the utmost importance that he should clearly apprehend, and (as opportunity serves) help the children to realise, the fundamental principle of the Christian attitude to prayer, particularly in so far as prayer takes the form of petition.[15]

The wise teacher, like 'the house-holder which bringeth forth out of his treasure things new and old', will use some prayers with which the children are thoroughly familiar, and in which all can join in saying, and some, which by their unfamiliarity will challenge thought and attention.[15]

(Here is inserted the addition on the nature of Christian prayer, and aspects of prayer and the practical suggestions.)

The Scripture Reading
(Here is nearly one page of comment.)

Recommended Books

The singing of hymns will always be one of the best forms of expression for the child's devotion and thanksgiving.

Hymns
(One page of practical hints and book suggestions.)

Hymns
(A brief note with suggestions of books.)

Prayers
(A four page collection of prayers.)

Prayers
(A two page note on types of prayer closing with books.)

The following notes show the most interesting points of difference between the 1924 and the 1939 articles.

1.   The 1924 version has four quotations from the New Testament. They are John 3.9; Mark 9.35; John 10.10 and Matt. 13.52. These express a spirit of liberal Christian idealism and optimism. All are omitted in 1939 which has instead a reference to the 'two greatest commandments' which are to become 'the basis of all the detailed instruction'. The inspirational is thus replaced by the instructional.

2.   The opening 1924 statement about the religious nature of all education is abbreviated in 1939. This point was now so secure that it needed no emphasis.

3.   Whereas the 1924 version hopes that all teaching will be 'infused with a sense of earnest enquiry', the 1939 version replaces this with 'infused with the appreciation of goodness, beauty and truth'. Again we note that questioning gives way to instruction. Goodness is Christian goodness; truth is Christian truth.

4.   The 1939 statement omits entirely the 1924 paragraph about experiential biblical teaching.

5.   The 1924 statement about the child learning by doing is expanded with emphasis upon the responsibility of the teacher for the spiritual moulding of the child. The section is set within an emphasis upon the all-encompassing guidance offered by the school. Here we see the growth of the idea of the state school as the instrument of Christian nurture.

6.   Whereas the 1924 syllabus addresses its questions

about Christian community to 'the school' the 1939 edition addresses itself to 'the Headmaster or Headmistress'.

7. The 1924 version asks whether the school encourages emulation and competition; the 1939 version is not so ready to regard competition as an evil. It speaks of 'proper forms of competition'.

8. The 1924 version speaks of the stronger helping the weaker but later this becomes 'the stronger and the cleverer'. Religious education was becoming more aware of itself as a grammar school subject, conscious of its role as an academic study for the able. Consistently, the 1924 reference to the need to submerge the pupil's desire to excel beneath teamwork and community service is omitted.

9. The 1924 version asks a rather courageous question about the prefectorial system. The prefects can be, it is suggested, 'little tyrants in the making'. This is entirely omitted in 1939.

10. With its greater confidence and (in some ways) its wider sense of international movements, the 1939 article adds the reference to the schools concern for 'wider causes'.

11. Instead of 'life abounding' as a mark of inspiration, 1939 has a question about teaching 'the grace of courtesy'. If the horizons are wider in 1939, the vision is duller.

12. It is highly significant that the 1924 paragraph about autonomy of the self in ethical judgments is replaced in 1939 with a paragraph about the biblical basis of ethics and discipline. The utilitarian ethics of 1924 ('every child thinks first of the common good') becomes the Christian ethics of 1939. See, for example, that in 1939 the 'common good' has become 'the charter of the common good' and the charter is the second great commandment. That in turn depends upon 'faith in the Father'.

13. The 1939 christological addition is also highly significant. Although the idea that Jesus did not rely on any external organization remains, his example is no longer described as being that of the great Teacher. Instead, we read of his 'unique personality', and this becomes the centre of the evangelistic ideal with which the passage concludes.

14. Whereas 1924 has but a brief paragraph on Morning Assembly, 1939 begins here with a new heading 'Corporate Prayer'. In the remarks which follow, the communal and

ethos building aspects of assembly are emphasized.

15.   In place of the comment about old and new prayers, supported rather incongruously by Matt. 13.52, the 1939 version adds a paragraph about the teacher's own example and adds a long essay on prayer and its meaning. Similarly the 1924 collection of prayers gives way to the 1939 essay on types of prayer.

Notes

Chapter 1

1. The expression 'Religious observances' was still in use in the 1930s and the expression 'School worship' did not become standard until the 1940s.

2. Rivingtons, 1850.

3. Circular 169 dated August 1878. See *Return: School Board Schools (Religious Teaching)*, House of Commons, 4 March 1879.

4. Circular 172 dated 5 February 1879. See *Return*, op.cit. Note that in 1888 there were 2225 School Boards. See J.W. Adamson, *English Education 1789-1902*, CUP 1930, p.365.

5. Ibid., pp. 163f. Denbigh School Board.

6. Ibid., p.164.

7. *Return: Education (Religious Education in Council Schools)*, 14 June 1906, HMSO.

8. From 1870 to 1944 schools maintained from public funds were permitted to teach religion but were not obliged to do so. What the schools actually did was thus within the discretion of the local authority or (in some cases) the head teacher. Full details of the situation may be found in Marjorie Cruickshank, *Church and State in English Education: 1870 to the present day*, Macmillan 1973, and James Murphy, *Church State and Schools in Britain, 1800-1970*, Routledge & Kegan Paul 1971. Note also that in England and Wales there are strictly speaking no state schools in that the centralized state does not own schools directly. Education has always been a responsibility of the local authorities who build, own and maintain the schools. Such schools have been known as Board Schools, Council Schools or Local Education Authority Schools, from time to time, depending on the structure of the local authority. They are also called County Schools and Maintained Schools. But in this book I sometimes call them state schools for the sake of simplicity.

9. See for a typical example, *Notes for Parents. A Syllabus Drawn up by the London Diocesan Council . . . with List of Recommended Books* with a preface by F.E. Ridgeway, Bishop of Kensington, Rivingtons 1908.

10. Diocese of Oxford, *List of lessons on the several steps in the Syllabus of Religious Instruction for Schools*, 1875; *The Syllabus of*

Religious Instruction for Schools, 1890; *Syllabus of Religious Instruction for use in the Diocese of Oxford*, 1903, and subsequent editions of 1905, 1910, 1918 and 1926. Yet further editions have followed.

11. Op.cit., 1918 ed., p.11.

12. *A Syllabus of a Course of Lessons suggested for use in Elementary Schools*, National Society's Depository, London 1901. The custom of associating 'Religious Observances and Instruction together at the beginning of the day was very persistent. See the 1937 West Riding Agreed Syllabus (p.v.). But the Surrey 1941 Syllabus makes a distinction (p.7). Note that the Education Act of 1921 restricted religious instruction to the beginning and ending of the school day. This is clearly due to the influence of the association between observances and instruction. Not until the 1944 Act could religion be taught at any time of the day, thus making it possible to have specialist teachers. Here lie the seeds of the distinction between worship and the classroom, a distinction which has come to a head today.

13. *A Syllabus of a Course of Lessons* . . ., p.23.

14. *Notes for Parents.* The full title of the Council in question is the London Diocesan Council for the Religious Education of the Children of the Wealthier Classes.

15. The roots of the new movement in religious education may be traced back at least as far as the 1910 Edinburgh Missionary Conference, when missionaries from many parts of the world reported that although converted peoples were able to repeat Christian words and actions, the basic structure of national life remained unchanged. This led to the movement for the 'Christianization of national life', a theme which was to feature in many ecumenical gatherings of the following decades. It then became clear that what was true abroad was true at home. Religious training was not enough; education of the whole personality was needed. Developments in the Sunday School in the early years of the century were another important influence, especially the work of the British Lessons Council and the influence of G.H. Archibald and the founding of Westhill College in 1907. See World Missionary Conference, 1910, *Report of Commission III, Education in Relation to the Christianization of National Life*; and Ethel A. Johnston, *George Hamilton Archibald, Crusader for Youth*, REP 1945.

16. *The Winchester Syllabus of Religious Instruction*, new ed. 1921. This is the Diocesan syllabus.

17. Ibid., p.5.

18. Loc.cit.

19. These short essays became particularly important in the series of syllabuses in the late 1960s: West Riding (1966), Lancashire (1968), London (1968) and others. When resource manuals were produced by Standing Advisory Committees for Religious Education (Cambridge, 1970) and by Advisers in Religious Education working with teachers' groups (*Interchange: Working Papers in Religious Education*, Essex Education Authority, 1970, duplicated), the essays became the materials from which the teachers would build their own syllabuses. See City of Bath Education Authority *Agreed Syllabus of Religious*

Education, 1970, for a syllabus which consists of nothing but a series of essays.

20. *The Winchester Syllabus of Religious Instruction*, new ed., 1921, p.9.

21. Ibid., p.27.

22. *Suggested Syllabus of Religious Instruction (Graded for children from 4 to 16 years of age). Drawn up in the light of more than five years practical use by some 3,000 teachers. For use in Council Schools*, Macmillan 1923, p.2.

23. Ibid., p.3.

24. Ibid., p.38.

25. *The Cambridgeshire Syllabus of Religious Teaching for Schools*, 1924, p.vi.

26. Ibid., p.1.

27. Instruction could only be saved by agreeing to exclude controversial elements. This thought did not, however, occur in the 1860s.

28. John Gellibrand Hubbard, *The Conscience Clause of the Education Department Illustrated from the Evidence taken by the Select Committee on Education*, 2nd ed., London 1865.

29. Ibid., p.8.

30. Ibid., p.14.

31. *Cambridgeshire Syllabus*, 1924, pp.1f.

32. Ibid., p.38.

33. See Appendix.

34. *The Cambridgeshire Syllabus of Religious Teaching for Schools*, rev. ed. 1939, pp. 24-26.

35. Ibid., p.40.

36. Ibid., pp. 83ff.

37. *The Cambridgeshire Syllabus of Religious Teaching for Schools*, 1949 ed., pp. 17ff.

38. Ibid., pp.46f; cf. 1939 ed., p.40.

39. Ibid., p.50. The influence of the Cambridgeshire syllabuses was remarkable. In 1940 more than 100 of the 317 Local Education Authorities were using either the 1924 or the 1939 editions. (Institute of Christian Education, *Religious Education in Schools. The Report of an Enquiry made by the Research Committee of the Institute of Christian Education into the Workings of the 1944 Education Act*, National Society/SPCK 1954, p.23.) This influence is, I suppose, due to the fact that the Cambridgeshire syllabuses were amongst the earliest of their kind, they were associated with a group of outstanding names (the 1924 committee included Alexander Nairn, W.B. Selbie, T.R. Glover, Sidney Cave, C. Anderson Scott, amongst several others), the 1924 syllabus is beautifully written (Sir Arthur Quiller-Couch was a member of the committee), but most important of all they captured the mood of the times, expressed what many teachers were feeling after, and offered leadership. After the 1944 Act many authorities prepared their own syllabuses and the predominance of Cambridge declined in this sense, but it continued to be widely quoted. Of the authorities who did

not compile their own syllabuses but adopted one from elsewhere, 23 adopted the Cambridgeshire syllabus and the same number the Sunderland syllabus. The Joint Four reported to the Research Committee of the ICE in 1954 that of the 580 grammar schools in their survey using agreed syllabuses, 113 were using the Cambridgeshire syllabus. Sunderland was used by 66 schools, Surrey by 53 and the West Riding by 50. (Information from *Religious Education in Schools*, pp.24 and 35.)

40. C.L. Berry, *The Teacher's Handbook to A Book of Morning Worship*, J.M. Dent 1946, p.11.

41. E.F. Braley, *The School without the Parson*, REP 1945, pp.7f.

42. *Oxford Book of School Worship* Parts II and III, SPCK, rev.ed. 1958, p.vi.

43. Ibid., p.v. This was a common assumption and had been so for years. 'No difference between Church schools, Council schools and Kindergartens has been made in this chapter. In the former, the Creed, the Gloria, the Sanctus or the Ave may be added, but the general remarks on School Prayer apply equally to all.' K.M. Penzer, *The Scripture Lesson in the Infant School and Kindergarten*, SCM Press 1935, p.96.

44. *Oxford Book of School Worship*, p.46.

45. Ibid., pp. 60-72.

46. Ibid., pp. xif.

47. Ibid., p.46.

48. Ibid., p.175.

49. Doris Starmer Smith, *The School Service*, REP 1945, p.8.

50. H.T. Salzer, *School Worship*, Institute of Christian Education 1952, 3rd ed., p.9.

51. Berry, op.cit., p.20.

52. Ibid., pp.22f.

53. Ibid., p.27.

54. Salzer, op.cit., p.4.

55. Ibid., p.5.

56. J.M. Macdougall Ferguson, *The School Assembly*, REP 1943; Doris Starmer Smith, op.cit.

57. In the 1958 *Oxford Book of School Worship* the prayer for the 'Death of a Pupil' attributes the death to 'thy fatherly care' and 'of thy goodness' (p.120). The prayers for the 'Death of a Member of Staff' (p.121) are somewhat less optimistic.

58. It would be difficult to find a more candid expression of pantheism than the poem by W.H. Carruth which one finds so often in the assembly anthologies, e.g. in H.F. Matthews, *A Book of Worship for Schools*, Epworth Press 1957, pp. 19ff.

59. e.g. D.M. Prescott, *The Senior Teacher's Assembly Book*, Blandford Press 1955, and more recently *More Readings for the Senior Assembly*, Blandford Press 1973.

60. I am describing general trends. The literature of school assembly during the period in question is extensive and exceptions to the trends are naturally to be found. J.T. Hilton, *Manual of Morning Worship*,

Schofield and Sims 1953, is a fairly manly selection for young secondaries and older juniors. We are mercifully spared any sentimental poetry and the selection of readings is stiffened by a good batch from classical authors and passages from the lives of great heroes. H.F. Matthews, in *A Book of Worship for Schools*, offers a generally sensible and mature collection and was probably the best book available in the fifties. Other examples which might interest the student of this odd corner of British educational literature are Josephine and Christine Bunch, *Prayers at School*, Lutterworth Press 1962, (typical of the earnest unimaginative type of service book); M.E. Jarvis, *Bible Readings and Prayers for a School Year*, SCM Press 1958 (busy head teacher's best friend; business-like equivalent to 'The Minister's Annual: Services and Sermons for a Year'; an unflinchingly conservative, orderly and thorough books), and J.D. Neil, *Morning Readings. A lectionary for schools*, Clowes 1963 (school worship becoming a hobby in its own right with eccentric results; odd combination of theological naivety with occasional learned asides; in the true nineteenth-century spirit of valuing Bible reading for itself without comment or explanation to the pupil).

61. E.g. West Riding, 1947, p.3.
62. E.g. Northumberland, 1948, p.18.
63. E.g. Burton-upon-Trent, 1948.
64. E.g. Durham, 1946, p.4.
65. E.g. Dorset, 1948, p.109.
66. Unfortunately, this work was not available at the time of writing.
67. E.g. Birmingham, 1952, p.10.
68. West Riding, 1937, p.xi.
69. Cambridgeshire, 1949, p.12.
70. London, 1947, p.21.
71. Ibid., p.25.
72. York, 1948, p.108.
73. Ibid., p.111.
74. Hertfordshire, 1954, p.11.
75. Lancashire, 1948, pp.101-107. The essay is by the then Bishop of Bradford, A.F.W. Blunt.
76. ' . . . religious education is education in religion, not merely in theory but also in practice. Domestic science or carpentry cannot be learned out of text-books, or even from oral instruction alone. Similarly a knowledge of how Christians have worshipped down the ages . . . is no substitute for training in the art of worship today. Not very much is included in this syllabus about school-worship, but that is because this was felt to be so vital a part of religious education that special and continued attention must be given to it.' County of Lincoln — Parts of Lindsey Education Committee: *Agreed Syllabus of Religious Instruction*, 1951, p.6.
77. *Religious Education in Schools*, p.24.
78. Reg and Evelyn Doidge, *Boys and Girls at Worship*, SCM Press 1965, is a good example. It is cheerful, certainly not stuffy or churchy, and although it contains no startling innovations, there are encouraging

little signs here and there.

79. OUP 1963.

80. Ibid., pp. 37-68.

81. Ibid., section III, pp.43f.

82. Since 1965 a great deal of practical progress has been made and the characteristics of the school assembly as indicated by the literature have undergone a transformation. School assembly is now much more alive to social, political and international issues and many schools are doing splendid work in creative use of drama and use of various media. Particular mention should be made of the work of John Bailey, Sheila Hobden, Ronald Dingwall and A.R. Bielby in encouraging lively and relevant assemblies. The 'Assembly Notebooks' in *Learning for Living* since 1972, contributed by Sheila Hobden, John Bailey and James Brimer contain many reports of work done in schools. But there has not been much reflection about the nature and purposes of the assembly, and in spite of the experimental work being done, in the majority of secondary schools the atmosphere and traditions of the forties and fifties continue.

Chapter 2

1. ' . . . the essential quality of worship, however simple or complex its form, is that it shall indeed be a conscious recognition of the worthship of God.' Westmorland Education Authority, *The Background of the Agreed Syllabus*, quoted in the West Riding Syllabus, 1947, p.3. 'There is a . . . case for the schools continuing to set before their members the worthiness of God by beginning the day with an act of worship.' R. Cant, 'The Nature of Worship' in *School Worship* ed. C.M. Jones, University of Leeds Institute of Education Paper no.3, 1965, p.11.

2. 'Christian worship is the giving to God of that which is His due, i.e. man's perfect love and obedience. This offering is made in response to all that God has shown Himself to be through Jesus Christ.' Exeter Education Committee, *Agreed Syllabus of Religious Instruction*, 1945, p.5.

3. 'Finally, let us remind ourselves that Christian worship is an affirmation of a Fact. We shall therefore seek to give proper place to the simple assumptions of Christian worship, i.e. that God is the Father of all men; that He has declared His will to us in the life and death and rising again of Jesus of Nazareth; that He continues to hold out His hand to those who will accept His living spirit today.' County Council of the West Riding of Yorkshire Education Department, *Syllabus of Religious Instruction*, March 1947, p.3.

4. 'We also worship Him when we use in the best way the gifts He has given us.' Exeter Education Committee, *Agreed Syllabus of Religious Instruction*, 1945, p.13.

5. ' . . . children can be trained to take part in corporate worship'. Exeter Education Committee, *Agreed Syllabus of Religious Instruction*, 1945, p.13, referring to Juniors aged 7 plus to 9. For an amusing

example of training in school worship, see the note 'Religious Education!' by Vernon Cornish in *Learning for Living*, November 1972, pp.28f.

6. 'A possible objection may be urged that the divided state of the Christian Church makes it impossible to teach the Christian religion, since different denominations hold such different views about the faith. If, however, the beliefs and practices peculiar to particular denominations are omitted, we are still left with a body of Christian teaching which contains essential features of supreme value. The Bible has a definite place in this scheme of instruction.' County Council of the West Riding of Yorkshire Education Department, *Syllabus of Religious Instruction*, March 1947, p.46.

7. 'Teachers undertaking the work of Religious Instruction are asked always to bear in mind:
1. That all teaching should be specifically Christian.
2. That Christian teaching accepts certain beliefs.
3. That as a matter of history these beliefs have been formulated in the Apostles' Creed . . .
4. That the essentials of belief may be stated in modern English thus: —
Christianity affirms — ' (a doctrinal statement follows).
City of Portsmouth Education Authority, *Syllabus of Religious Instruction*, 1952, p.15.

8. The history of discussion as a method in religious education supports this conclusion. Discussion was frowned upon in the nineteenth century. Caroline Fry, in her *Scripture Principles of Education*, wrote in 1833: 'Independence of opinion is not a grace; it is a vice . . . if I wished to produce in manhood a proud free thinker, or a lawless democrat, this is the method I would use; but not if I desired to see in my child a humbly, believing, self-distrusting child of God.' The point is reinforced by a discussion of the dangers of discussion in religious education (pp.67f. and 85ff.). Contrast this with the comment from the 1924 Cambridgeshire Syllabus which, as we have seen, marked the dawn of liberalism in religious education. 'Every teacher knows how we learn by teaching; he knows it better than his father did. Authority gave place to teaching, and today teaching gives place to conversation' (p.3). It is interesting to see that this statement, with its emphasis upon mutual learning rather than teacher-directed instruction was omitted from many of the later syllabuses, which also abandoned 'Religious Teaching' and reverted to the wording 'Religious Instruction' in their titles.

9. It was thus a 'daring venture' to indicate to pupils even in senior forms that there were other religions and philosophies or that the Christian faith itself presented difficulties. When this was done, it was only for apologetic purposes. 'This has involved us in a daring venture into the philosophy of religion, but we were convinced that on or even before leaving school the pupil today is brought up against ideologies, or unformulated modes of thought, essentially opposed to the Christian world-view, and would be incapable of dealing with them without some

knowledge of the basic assumptions about God, man, and the universe which Christianity makes.' County of Lincoln — Parts of Lindsey Education Committee, *Agreed Syllabus of Religious Instruction*, 1951, p.9. '. . . the moral problems of the Old Testament form one of the principal points of attack on Christianity itself; and children should be fore-armed, especially in their last terms, against the criticism they will inevitably hear upon leaving school.' City of Nottingham Education Committee, *Suggestions for Schemes of Religious Instruction*, 1940, p.11. An interesting example of discussion within an instructional frame of reference is found in the 1952 Portsmouth Agreed Syllabus. The possibility of discussion arose from the fact that 'As the children grow older, questions will be asked upon the answer to which there may be a wide variety of opinion.' The reaction of the Syllabus to this situation is that the teacher is still the answerer, and 'in answering such questions the teacher makes it clear that he or she is expressing a personal opinion . . .' But no attempt should be made to stimulate such questions, nor should any attempt be made to prevent them arising. '. . . there seems little point in setting aside time for the raising of doubts or difficulties which may never have occurred to the children' (p.99).

10. For the pressures upon social groups who hold beliefs not shared by most of their neighbours, see L. Festinger, *A Theory of Cognitive Dissonance*, 1957 and P.L. Berger and T. Luckmann, *The Social Construction of Reality*, Penguin 1967.

11. As the reader is aware, by 'instruction' I mean much more than the giving of information. Naturally an educated choice cannot precede knowledge of the facts about which choice is to be made. But educated choice should precede enrolment in instruction which assumes the facts to be true and presents no others.

12. e.g. Australia and New Zealand.

13. Horace Bushnell, *Christian Nurture*, Yale University Press 1967, is the classic expression of Protestant nurture. Written in 1861, the book sets out nurture as intending 'that the child is to grow up a Christian, and never know himself as being otherwise' (p.4). For more recent discussion see Wayne R. Rood, *On Nurturing Christians*, Abingdon Press, Nashville, Tenn. 1972 and D.G. Butler, *Religious Education, The Foundations and Practice of Nurture*, Harper & Row, NY 1962.

14. For 'catechesis of experience' see The Higher Institute of Catechetics of Nijmegen (Holland), *Fundamentals and Programmes of a New Catechesis*, Duquesne University Press, Pittsburgh 1967, pp.88ff.

Chapter 3

1. See my article 'The Integration of Religious Education and Some Problems of Authority', *Religious Education in Integrated Studies* ed. Ian H. Birnie, SCM Press 1972.

2. For a discussion of the educational value of worship from a critical period in the development of school worship, see D.R.

Richardson 'The educational value of public divine worship', in *Modern Christian Education*, Vol. XXVIII, nos. 5, 6, and 7, of *The Modern Churchman*, 1938, pp.343-356. The discussion is not related to the school situation and is argued mainly in terms of a Platonic understanding of worship and educational values.

3. James N. Brown, *Educational Implications of Four Conceptions of Human Nature*, Catholic University of America Press, Washington 1940.

4. Paulo Freire, *Pedagogy of the Oppressed*, Penguin 1972.

5. Ray L. Hart, *Unfinished Man and the Imagination*, Herder & Herder, NY 1968.

6. Ibid., pp.188ff.

7. This is clearly brought out by the history, in the Greek Bible and in early Christian thought, of the term. See *Theological Dictionary of the New Testament* ed. G. Kittel and G. Friedrich, Wm B. Eerdmans, Michigan 1968 and SCM Press, Vol. V, article on Παιδεία. The educational writings of Martin Buber are also relevant to this aspect. See his *Between Man and Man*, Fontana 1971.

8. Paulo Freire's work is outstanding in its emphasis upon reading as an anthropological task and not merely a technique.

9. Gabriel Moran, *Design for Religion*, Search Press 1970, p.120.

10. The distinction between Christian education and Christian nurture was sometimes realized even in the midst of what we have described as the high point of nurture. ' . . . the vital topic of personal religion. It should be a by-product of our lessons, not a deliberate objective. The Scripture lesson is neither a sermon nor an act of worship. For both of these there is a place in school life, but that place is not the classroom.' J.T. Christie, 'What is Christian Education?' in the City of Portsmouth Education Authority, *Syllabus of Religious Instruction*, 1952, p.11.

11. This flows from the biblical understandings of history and is thus an insight about education shared by Judaism and Christianity. See Martin Buber, 'Teaching and Deed', *Israel and the World*, Schocken Books, NY 1963, p.139.

Chapter 4

1. E.L. Edmond, *The School Inspector*, Routledge & Kegan Paul 1962, pp.1ff.

2. Ibid., p.7.

3. Ibid., p.84.

4. Ibid., p.104.

5. Ibid., p.115.

6. *The Yearbook of Education*, 1932, ed. Lord Eustace Percy, p.260.

7. *Church Assembly: Report of the Commission on Religious Education*, 1929, p.86.

8. *Yearbook of Education*, p.261.

9. Editorial in *The Schoolmaster*, 24 October 1940.

10. Canon E.F. Braley, *A Policy in Religious Education*, 1941, p.82.

11. The *Spens Report*, 1938, p.215.

12. Braley, op. cit.

13. The following is an example of the nurturing intention of the sponsoring relationship which the church took towards religious education, and of the role of school worship: 'It is also hoped that the atmosphere of school-worship, and the new approach to religious instruction will increasingly lead pupils to become and remain full members of a worshipping community outside the school. If it does not, we should judge that as religious education it had failed.' County of Lincoln — Parts of Lindsey Education Committee, *Agreed Syllabus of Religious Instruction*, 1951, p.6.

14. Spencer Leeson, *Christian Education* (Bampton Lectures for 1946), Longmans 1947; *Christian Education Reviewed*, Longmans 1957.

15. ' . . . the agreed syllabuses from 1940 onwards reveal a great change of emphasis. Increasing attention is paid in them to worship and the aim of the teaching is declared to be that children should understand and accept the Christian faith and follow the Christian way of life, while in more recent syllabuses the hope is expressed that school worship and religious instruction will, in the words of the Introduction to the Lindsey syllabus, "increasingly lead pupils to become and remain full members of a worshipping community outside the school".' Institute of Christian Education, *Religious Education in Schools*, 1954, p.27.

16. This may be illustrated by two excerpts from the influential and widely used Sunderland Syllabus: ' . . . the School ought to do its positive best to guide children into Church membership, just as it would guide them into the Continuation School'. Lord Eustace Percy, 'Foreword' in the County Borough of Sunderland Education Committee, *Syllabus of Religious Instruction*, 1944, p.8. 'This syllabus . . . provides material by which the attempt can be made to direct the teaching of Religious Knowledge into the teaching of Religion, that is, a personal relationship between the learner and God . . .', ibid., p.5.

17. See Sunderland, 1944, p.5. This is typical.

18. Schools Council Working Papers 36 and 44 are examples of curriculum influences by-passing the Agreed Syllabus.

19. It is still possible for an official Agreed Syllabus to carry considerable prestige and thus to mould practice and opinion within religious education. The 1975 Birmingham Syllabus (awaiting publication) is the outstanding example. But from the start, it was recognized by many of the participants that this was not the most effective nor most proper way to effect classroom change. See my article 'Agreed Syllabuses, past, present and future' in the symposium *New Movements in Religious Education* ed. Ninian Smart and Donald Horder, Maurice Temple Smith 1975.

20. Harold Loukes, *New Ground in Christian Education*, SCM Press 1965, is about religious education in state schools. Nobody today could write a book on such a subject with such a title.

21. e.g. G.E. Phillips, 'The study of other religions in schools', *Religion in Education*, Vol. VI, October 1939, pp.221ff.

22. In the terminology of the '40s and '50s religious education is the whole of education as (Christianly) nurturing the whole person and religious instruction is the subject of the curriculum. Both were nurturing activities and RI was part of a larger RE. The later distinction between RE (subject) and CE (overall nurturing purpose, or subject taught with nurturing intention) is not a very helpful one. It is better to speak of RE and CN (Christian Nurture), reserving the expression CE for critical enquiring education as supported by (but not serving the immediate interests of) Christian faith.

In the Portsmouth Agreed Syllabus of 1952, J.T. Christie distinguished Christian instruction (teaching the content of Christian faith and history) from Christian education (life-long nurture in Christian character and faith). 'Christian education is a wider and deeper thing than instruction in Christianity — it is a training for a way of life' (p.8). Christian instruction is merely the name of a school subject. Christie also draws a distinction between the aims of this instruction (the scripture lesson) and the worship and cultivation of personal religion (p.11). See above, chapter 3, note 10.

23. I have discussed the significance of the withdrawal clauses in my contribution to Birnie, op.cit., pp.86-89.

24. See my article 'Religious education in a pluralist society' in the symposium edited by Monica J. Taylor and to be published in 1975 by the National Foundation for Educational Research, Slough.

25. I choose Islam simply as a great religion relevant to British schools. The same points could be made, however, by contrasting certain forms of Christianity with other forms of Christianity.

26. I discuss the criteria (the material principles) for including secular ideologies within religious education syllabuses in Taylor, op.cit. See also my editorial in *Learning for Living*, September 1974.

27. I am thinking, e.g., that Christian iconography might give rise to use of a kind of visual method which would not be so useful in teaching Islam when there is caligraphy rather than iconography.

28. *Learning for Life*, Agreed Syllabus of the Inner London Education Authority, 1968, p.13.

29. The unanimous faith of the school community as expressed through the assembly is a frequent motif in the Agreed Syllabuses. Assembly is 'a formal act or demonstration whereby the school community expresses its faith, acknowledges its loyalty and affirms the nature of the spiritual bond which binds its members together'. City of York Education Committee, *City of York Agreed Syllabus of Religious Instruction*, 1948, p.108.

30. J.G. Williams, *Worship and the Modern Child*, SPCK 1951, p.147.

31. Ibid., p.149.

32. Ibid., p.172.

33. Ibid., p.151. The final word is, significantly, put into quotation marks by Williams.

34. Ibid.; footnote on p.152, quoting M.V.C. Jeffreys.

35. Although seldom spelt out as clearly as in Williams' book, this aspect of school worship is often mentioned in the syllabuses. 'If properly conducted, this (corporate worship) should be the most influential feature of the religious teaching of a school.' County of Lincoln — Parts of Lindsey Education Committee, *Agreed Syllabus of Religious Instruction*, 1951, p.10. It is also interesting and indicative of the deep hold which this sort of thing has in the minds of otherwise progressive educators, that J.G. Williams' argument is quoted with approval in the West Riding Religious Education Agreed Syllabus of 1966 (*Suggestions for Religious Education*, p.117).

36. *The Fourth R: The Report of the Commission on Religious Education in Schools*, National Society/SPCK 1970, para. 297.

37. Ibid., paras. 112-116 and 201-218.

38. Ibid., para. 297.

39. Ibid., para. 117.

40. Ibid., para. 138.

41. Ibid., para. 185.

42. Ibid., para. 113.

43. Ibid., para. 213.

44. Ibid., paras 246-248.

45. Ibid., para. 215.

46. Ibid., para. 117.

47. Loc.cit.

48. Ibid., para. 217.

49. Ibid., para. 309.

50. Ibid., para. 117, quoting Ninian Smart.

51. Ibid., para. 295.

52. Ibid., para. 298.

53. Loc.cit. This understanding of worship is consistent with what we have seen in our chapter 2 above. That worship so understood assumes the truth of certain Christian doctrines is maintained not only by secularists but by Christians as diverse as J.G. Williams and myself.

54. Ibid., para. 113.

55. Ibid., para. 248.

56. Ibid., para. 296.

57. Loc.cit.

58. Loc.cit. This comment is probably intended as the 'easement of conscience' which is referred to in para. 317.

59. Ibid., paras. 299 and 300.

60. Ibid., para. 298.

61. Ibid., para. 296.

62. It is interesting to see that in para. 357 the practice of confirmation in independent schools is described as having 'been all too often . . . a ceremony undergone by almost all pupils, whatever degree of Christian commitment they have reached'. Exactly the same should have been said of school worship.

63. Christians should not allow themselves to be comforted by the thought that, after all, 'you cannot compel a person to worship since

worship is an inward thing'. Tell that to a Christian when compelled to offer incense to Caesar.

64. Op. cit., paras. 136f.

65. See the discussion of openness in paras. 248 and 298.

66. The daily act of worship is 'a doing rather than a learning'. City of York Education Committee, *The City of York Agreed Syllabus of Religious Instruction*, 1948, p.108.

67. I owe this observation to Robin Richardson's article 'Images of God: Some Notes on School Worship', *Learning for Living*, May 1972, pp.19-22.

68. Ibid., p.21.

69. C.Z. Nunn, 'Child control through a "coalition with God"', *Child Development*, 35 (1964), pp. 417-432.

Chapter 5

1. Horace Bushnell, *Christian Nurture*, Yale University Press 1967, p.4.

2. Gabriel Moran, *Design for Religion*, Search Press 1971, p.17.

3. There is, of course, no reason why state schools should not, if they wish, offer facilities for individual or voluntary groups of pupils to worship. The use of 'quiet' rooms in Leicestershire schools is a case in point. But the facilities will not be confined to *Christian* worship and the state school has no exact duty to its clients to offer these facilities, except in so far as they might form part of the provisions for an effective religious education department.

4. 1 Samuel 16.7.

5. Paul Tillich, 'Existentialist Aspects of Modern Art', *Christianity and the Existentialists*, ed. Carl Michalson, Charles Scribner's Sons, NY 1956, pp. 128-147.

6. It is the form of the literature which makes it art, and transformation is achieved through encounter with another form. But literature is speech-art and so the rational, overt content has a significance which it lacks in non-verbal art forms.

Chapter 6

1. I think we might distinguish the values and beliefs which a school should demonstrate and discuss from those which it should discuss but not demonstrate. There is, however, no simple way in which values and beliefs can be placed neatly in one box or the other.

2. This is of course not a new idea. '. . . a morning assembly without any specifically religious content would be a valuable feature in the life of the school'. London County Council, *The London Syllabus of Religious Education*, 1947, p.22.

3. James Brimer, 'School Worship with Juniors', *Learning for Living*, May 1972, pp.6-12.

4. I have briefly discussed the question of integrating the curriculum through the school assembly in my article in Birnie, op. cit., pp.94.

School assembly has had this integrating function since the early thirties, but the basis of the integration was theological and required unanimity of religious belief on the part of the school community. 'In worship the whole life of the individual and the community is offered to God, in the knowledge and service of whom are found the meaning and the unity of all the experiences and activities that life can hold' (Institute of Christian Education, *Religious Education in Schools*, 1954, p.89). 'It is the Divine Being met with in such services who gives meaning to all subjects of instruction, and provides sanction and justification for all that is taught and felt to be of good report in daily experience' (M.L. Jacks, *God in Education*, 1939, p.176).

5. I once had the unusual experience of a mathematics department in a secondary school protesting because they had not been asked to take part in a series of assemblies on 'What the subjects say about war'. 'How can you have war without computers?' they said, 'and how can you have computers without mathematicians?'

6. Attributed to King Henry VI (1421-1471).

7. Attributed to William Bright (1824-1901).

8. The fine work of John Bailey, the Religious Education Adviser for Lincolnshire, should be noticed. A number of collections of hymns and songs written by teachers and pupils have been prepared under his direction.

Index

Proper names are given in italics